OXFORD WORCESTER
& WOLVERHAMPTON

PORTRAIT OF A FAMOUS ROUTE

Part One: Oxford to Worcester

BOB PIXTON

This pictorial work on the Oxford-Worcester-Wolverhampton route is published in two parts:
Part One herewith covers the line from Oxford to Worcester.
Part Two will cover the line from Worcester to Wolverhampton.
The whole comprises around three hundred photographs, mainly from the steam era, forming a comprehensive record of this fascinating, vitally important and very busy part of the British railway system.

0131822561

RU...SHING

Front cover: 'Castle' class 4-6-0 No.7007 *Great Western* makes a rousing start out of Worcester on a London-bound express. Worcester's 'Castles', such as No.7007, were renowned for their clean condition.   *Unknown*

Back cover – top: A busy scene on the southern approach to Oxford station in the late 1940s, with a goodly variety of motive power on view.   *Author's collection*

Back cover – middle: Honeybourne Junction, in rural surroundings, witnesses the passage of an immaculate 'Castle' on a down express.   *A W V Mace Collection / Mile Post 92 1/2 Picture Library*

Back cover – bottom: The northern end of the Oxford Worcester & Wolverhampton is seen in GWR days. Wolverhampton will be covered in Part Two of this book.

Additional text and illustrations concerning Oxford, Cotswold Country and Cathedral Line
kindly provided by Alan Bennett on pages 10-13; 53-55; 82-83.

© 2003 Bob Pixton

Published by Runpast Publishing, 10 Kingscote Grove, Cheltenham, Gloucestershire GL51 6JX

Typesetting and reproduction by Viners Wood Associates – 01452 812813
Printed in England by The Amadeus Press Ltd., Cleckheaton

ISBN 1 870754 59 X

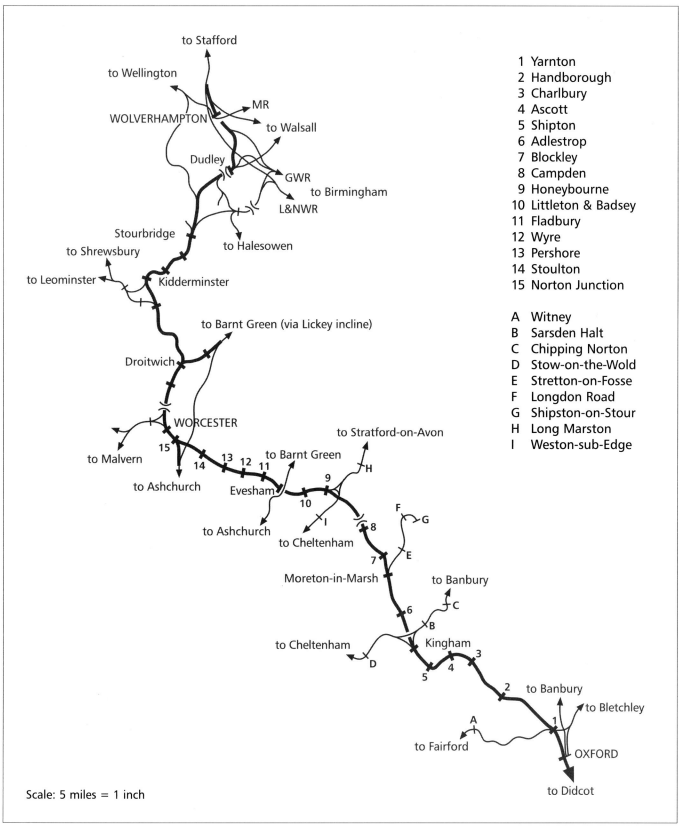

to Stafford

to Wellington

WOLVERHAMPTON

MR

to Walsall

Dudley

GWR

to Birmingham

L&NWR

Stourbridge

to Halesowen

to Shrewsbury

to Leominster

Kidderminster

to Barnt Green (via Lickey incline)

Droitwich

WORCESTER

to Stratford-on-Avon

to Malvern

15

14   13   12   11

to Barnt Green

to Ashchurch

Evesham

10

9

H

to Ashchurch

I

F

G

to Cheltenham

8

E

7

Moreton-in-Marsh

to Banbury

6

B

C

to Cheltenham

Kingham

D

5   4   3

2

to Banbury

A

1

to Bletchley

to Fairford

OXFORD

to Didcot

Scale: 5 miles = 1 inch

1 Yarnton
2 Handborough
3 Charlbury
4 Ascott
5 Shipton
6 Adlestrop
7 Blockley
8 Campden
9 Honeybourne
10 Littleton & Badsey
11 Fladbury
12 Wyre
13 Pershore
14 Stoulton
15 Norton Junction

A Witney
B Sarsden Halt
C Chipping Norton
D Stow-on-the-Wold
E Stretton-on-Fosse
F Longdon Road
G Shipston-on-Stour
H Long Marston
I Weston-sub-Edge

This map shows the OWW route with main connections. The distance from Oxford to Worcester is fifty-seven miles; from Worcester to Wolverhampton is thirty-three and a half miles.

A splendid portrait at Campden which encapsulates the bygone era nearly a century ago as GWR steam railmotor No.69 pauses on its journey. This vehicle, incorporating a small steam engine unit in a passenger coach, was built in 1906. The GWR eventually had 99 steam rail motors, but they were not ideal, being prone to vibration, and dirt from the engine's coal made it difficult to keep the passenger compartment clean. Furthermore, their capacity was limited as passenger numbers rose. So many, including this one, were converted from the 1920s to trailer coaches hauled by conventional steam locomotives.

Lens of Sutton

Introduction

Oxford Worcester & Wolverhampton Railway.
On 4 August 1845 the Oxford Worcester & Wolverhampton Railway Company was empowered to build a line from the Oxford branch of the Great Western Railway, through Evesham and Worcester to meet the Grand Junction Railway at Wolverhampton. Branches were planned to the River Severn at Worcester, to the Birmingham & Gloucester at Stoke Prior, from Amblecote at Stourbridge and from Oak Farm, Kingswinford to Brettell Lane. A further connection at Abbots Wood to Worcester would enable that city to be approached from both Gloucester in the south and Birmingham in the north.

The main purpose of the line was to serve as a competitor to the well established London to Birmingham Railway which was thought by users to be abusing its monopoly of fast transport between the two most important cities in England at the time. Being supported by the GWR it would provide an opportunity for that company to expand into this lucrative market.

One line, two different areas.
On its course from Oxford, through Worcester to Wolverhampton, the line takes on different characteristics according to the area. The city of Oxford always has been an important meeting place while the county is predominantly agricultural. After the barrier of the Cotswolds has been penetrated, the market garden of the Vale of Evesham leads to the historically important city of Worcester. North and the waters of Droitwich give way to light industry around Kidderminster. Beyond is the 'Black Country' with its glass making at Stourbridge then onto heavy steel making at Round Oak and elsewhere, and the extensive manufacturing industries of the West Midlands. So the southern part of the line served historical and agricultural places, with the northern part serving industries.

The southern part.
The north-eastern part of Oxfordshire, with minor forays into Gloucestershire, has been prevented, as if by fate, from ever attaining the position of a great industrial or commercial centre. The area that the line passes through is rather especially adapted to the requirements and practise of agriculture. There is little or nothing in the area that would necessarily create an industrial district. There are a small number of enterprises that have developed, based on localised natural resources. The qualities of the water in the River Windrush enabled blanket making to thrive in the west and iron ore was discovered in the north from the mid 1850s. Many parts of the area have seen the geology exploited in stone quarries and in brick making. Except for these, the area has no natural reasons for being an industrial area. Most of the trades have arisen from domestic industries, or from the needs of Oxford as a university town.

North-west of the Cotswolds and the fertile Vale of Evesham in Worcestershire is passed through. Protection by the surrounding hills, having the advantage of deposits from the River Severn in geological times and being well draining combined together to give the area an advantage in growing certain vegetables and fruit. The Midland Railway with its north-south line from Gloucester to Birmingham really only passed the fringes of the vale and so there existed the opportunity for an east-west line through the area.

The GWR promoted this section heavily and tried to celebrate the rural traditions of the area. The GWR produced much literature on the area – 'Cotswold Ways' in 1924; 'The Cotswold Country' in 1936 and in its GWR Magazine emphasised 'Holiday Haunts', all highlighting the Englishness of the towns. Chipping Campden and Burford were extensively written about in impressionistic tones. The Vale of Evesham was dubbed 'The Garden of England' by the GWR General Manager, James Inglis, in 1904, and 1929's 'Holiday Haunts' waxed lyrical about Pershore's plums. Evesham itself was described as one of the 'most historical towns in the Midlands'. The company considered Worcester to be 'one of the oldest, proudest and most interesting towns in the Midlands' declaring the city to be 'one of the Empire's foremost travel shrines'. Again, Englishness was promulgated with the cathedral being the focal point, aided by the Royal Worcester Porcelain and the annual Hop & Ram fair – the latter two having long historical connections as was pointed out to tourists.

Contents

Above: **South of Oxford, 1950s**. This view is towards Oxford station along the down slow line. Off to the right the branch to Princes Risborough departs at Kennington Junction. In the background can be made out 'Redbridge' – the pleasing lines of the central part of the bridge contrast to the concrete block arches for the up and down goods lines. These were part of the wartime programme to improve traffic facilities and flow on this important route to the south coast from the Midlands and the north. Millstream Junction, where the line to Banbury left the original branch, was just under the bridge. On the up goods running loop is 2-6-0 No.5332 being overtaken by an unidentified 2-6-2T on the up main. *Author's collection*

Below: **Hinksey South, 1950s**. Looking north from the road bridge shows the start of Hinksey Yard. It was constructed in 1941-2, much of it by Italian POWs and involved the elevation of the line by several feet and culverting several streams passing across the area. There were two shunting spurs, No.1 is on the right, to allow two lots of sorting to go on independently. The controlling signal box, brought into use on 29 March 1942, had 14" thick walls and a 12" reinforced concrete roof designed to withstand bomb blasts; there was a similar one on the down side at the end of the yard. It was to the right that the original line went from Millstream Junction to the first station in Oxford. *Author's collection*

Above: **Osney Lane footbridge, 19 July 1965.** A public footpath links Osney, a working class district of west Oxford, with the St Thomas district, east of the railway line, leading to the castle, prison and the town centre. It crosses the main running lines and sidings (now the station car park) on a footbridge. In the last few months of steam working, 0-6-0PT No.9789 trundles an up transfer freight towards Hinksey. The signal box, Oxford Station South, was formerly called Oxford Goods Shed. It had a brick skirt added as a wartime protective measure in 1942. *A Swain*

Below: **Osney Lane footbridge, late 1940s.** The passenger station is again in the background with its rectangular water tank north of the Botley Road and a parachute tank to the south. Waiting to back onto coaches in the up platform is an SR Bulleid 'Pacific' with that region's distinct headcode discs. On the down side, the station pilot, having waited in the 'West Midland Sidings' on the left, has backed onto the recent arrival and is about to add a van. Beckett Street goods yard is on the right, the picture showing the impressive ladder-like connections to it. Waiting in the up goods loop is an ex-LNWR 0-8-0 with a train of empty mineral wagons; when a path becomes clear it will set off along the ladder to the down through line on its way north, probably to Bletchley. In the next siding is a GWR engine waiting to bring its coaches into the station. *Author's collection*

Above: **Oxford Station South, 1957**. This view is south from the end of the up platform. The first point on the left allows up trains to pass from the platform to the up main line, while a short distance further on the second point enables exchange engines to await their train. The last wagons of the freight are passing under Beckett Street (Osney Lane) footbridge while the engine, GWR 2-8-0 2800 class No.3842, passes over Botley Road on the down main line and will pass through the station. The slight rising gradient is detectable. Note the steps to the signal box are at the back, space presumably restricting its siting at the more conventional end. This box, and all those between Radley (up line) / Culham (down line), to the south, and Heyford, in the north, as well as the former OWW as far as Ascott-under-Wychwood were replaced by the Oxford panel situated on the down platform in October 1984. The wooden sleepers by the engine allow road vehicles, too tall for the restricted bridge under the line (13' 6"), to cross the line.   *Author's collection*

Below: **Oxford station, exterior, early 1950s**. Classic car enthusiasts would have a field day with these cars. While the overall roof was removed some sixty years earlier, most of the structures here making up the original station were about one hundred years old! Both up and down platforms were accessed by roads from Botley Road, either side of the underbridge; passengers could walk from one to the other by means of a subway. When the station first opened, there were separate waiting rooms for different classes of passengers.   *David Lawrence*

Oxford

It is easy to overlook, given our current mobility and populated land, the situation that existed just before railways burst upon the scene. Important as a market town, river and road centre and the seat of the diocese & county town, Oxford was the sixth largest town in the land with a population of about one thousand around the time of the Norman conquest. The cloth trade that had led to its growth was in decline from the Middle Ages. However, by the time of the first railway links, though the population had grown to about 25,000, Oxford's ranking had slipped so that now it was probably about the sixtieth town in the land.

It is tempting to believe that the present station in Oxford is the result of careful siting and continuous upgrading over the last 150 years. However, this view ignores the influences on early railways by vested interests: Oxford was, and still is, rife with such. Thus it was that Christ Church College, as a major land owner, successfully opposed the Oxford Railway's plans to have a station alongside Cowley Road. The City Council, collectors of the not inconsiderable tolls from the Folly Bridge over the River Thames, also objected to that bridge being rebuilt. Thus successive plans in 1837/38 & 1840 were lost in the House of Lords. Other interested parties also collaborated to try to stop the railway. The Oxford Canal Company, not surprisingly, was looking after its shareholder's interests in objecting while the Chancellor of the University, the Duke of Wellington, was against such enterprises as it would encourage the lower orders to move about. In fact the morals of the students were uppermost in the University's thoughts as it didn't want them to go to places like Ascot, although it accepted the need for travel. After various accommodations with objectors, an Act was passed in 1843; amalgamation with the funding provider, the broad gauge GWR, and opening of the railway took place in June 1844.

The just under ten mile branch was from the main line at Didcot and terminated south of the river, west of the Folly Bridge, some distance from the city. Across the river was Oxford gas works, established there since 1818. Passengers were accommodated in a single platform wooden station while goods facilities, still of wooden construction, were much larger, but it all appeared rather cheap, as if there was no certainty that the railway would last. An Act of Parliament in 1845 authorised the construction of a line north towards Rugby, but not as an extension of the branch from Didcot; it would be another five years before the first part was opened to Banbury. This line departed from the original branch around milepost 62 from London. It crossed the river, the main road to the west, the Sheepwash Channel (a branch of the Thames linking the river to the Oxford canal) before heading north and was opened on 2 September 1850. Gravel excavated to provide some ballast for the

OXFORD
SEE BRITAIN BY TRAIN

line came from the fields in the 'V' between it and the original line: the resultant Hinksey Lakes were bought by the city as a reservoir.

The site chosen for Oxford's through station was just north of the main road west (now Botley Road); construction of the wooden buildings meant that it was not ready for almost two years after the line opened. This necessitated passenger trains passing south, through the emerging station, to the junction with the original line at Millstream, and then reversing into the station at Grandpont, with a similar situation existing for northbound trains. This situation persisted until the new station opened in October 1852, the original one handling goods only until closure in 1872, the current houses there dating some fifteen years or so afterwards. While all this was happening, in 1851, the rival LNWR opened its Rewley Road terminus on its line from Bletchley, adjacent to the soon to be opened new GWR station. The latter was to consist of two central through lines, flanked by up and down platform faces, all under a large train shed with glazed ends, an enlarged version of the one at Banbury. A rebuilding of the GWR station, almost forty years later swept away the overall roof, refurbished the subway and resulted in progressive enlargement of the platforms until 1910. The wooden buildings were easily demolished in 1970, paved the way for a new £3 million station to open in 1990.

Land adjacent to the station at Cripley Meadow was the subject of plans in 1865 to build a carriage & wagon works. Swindon was reported to the GWR directors as being 'wholly out of the question as there was no narrow gauge there'. Oxford alone was suitable in every way, being central and having broad and narrow gauge accommodation and needing between 3-400 skilled workers. Again, the vested interests of the University combined to defeat the plans which, ironically, were put into operation at ... Swindon!

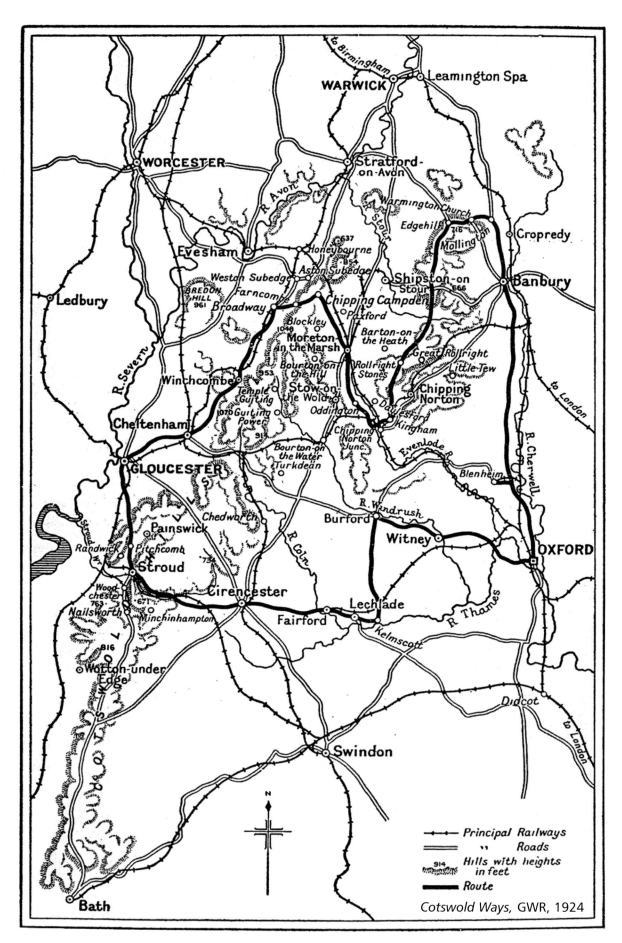

Cotswold Ways, GWR, 1924

Oxford, Cotswold Country & Cathedral Line

The GWR route from Oxford through the Cotswolds to Worcester was illustrative of three vital elements in the company's promotional work, both literary and visual. From 1904 and the publication of 'Historic Sites And Scenes Of England', dedicated to "The Travellers of All Nations", the company proclaimed its extensive historical and cultural credentials together with its deep and directly related identification with traditional, rural England. Oxford, Worcester, Evesham and the widespread Cotswold landscape of field, village and town, for example, fulfilled all three categories unreservedly, and were thus the focus of a direct appeal to both home and overseas visitors alike, particularly American tourists looking to ancestral links.

Oxford

Oxford had immense historical and cultural resonance internationally whilst in a regional context the GWR characterised it as the south-eastern gateway to the Cotswolds with its direct access from London. The River Thames also offered an alternative perspective with the company's promotion of combined river-rail excursions between Oxford, Wallingford, Reading, Windsor and London.

'Oxford and Shakespeare Land', 1928, described the city as one "of old grey walls and lovely gardens, of Colleges and ancient Churches, in which a large part of the history of England is written." Town, Colleges and Chapels had "grown together in picturesque disorder" [whilst] "the University itself is redolent of the names of men famous in religion, commerce, law and education; in war and peace; and, in fact, in every phase of human activity". This was the message in 'Oxford and Shake-speare-Land' published by the GWR, primarily for the American market, in 1928 as one of its 'Handy Aid' series. 'Holiday Haunts' also stressed the city's historic identity: "Oxford was a powerful town in Saxon times. The royal palace of Beaumont, which was the scene of many important gatherings has long since vanished, but the church of St Peter-in-the-East, believed to be one of the oldest surviving churches in England, and the tower of St Michael's are all relics of those far-off days..." Whilst it devoted extensive coverage to the University in all its aspects, 'Holiday Haunts' also put the city's wider history into a national context, indicating its relative neglect, in guide books generally:

... all the splendour of Oxford's early importance, and all the interest in the Saxon and Norman relics, which would be a proud adornment to any other city, never gain more than a secondary interest from tourists.

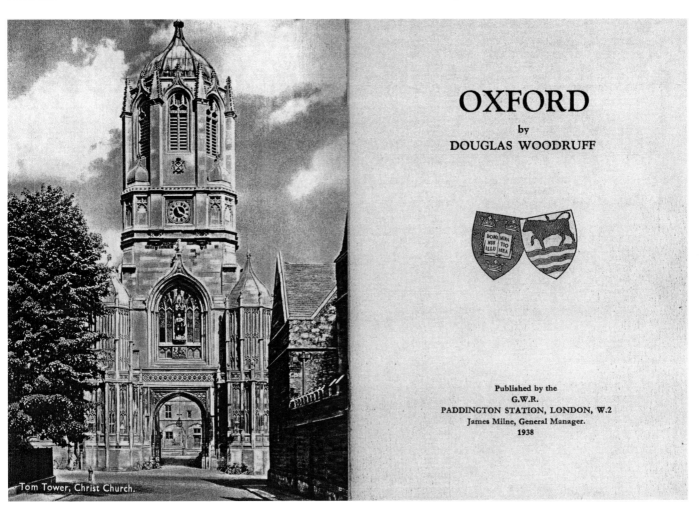

Tom Tower, Christ Church.

OXFORD

by
DOUGLAS WOODRUFF

Published by the
G.W.R.
PADDINGTON STATION, LONDON, W.2
James Milne, General Manager.
1938

Above: Sheldonian Theatre and Bodleian Library from *Oxford,* 1938.

Below: City of Dreaming Spires from *Oxford,* 1938.

'England And Why', a joint publication by the GWR and the Southern Railway, again, for the American market, underlined Oxford's international reputation. In a somewhat different comparative category, the 1931 edition of 'England And Why' considered Oxford as "a formidable rival to London", and further, that, in its international perspective, "Oxford claims to rank with Rome as a City of Palaces". Its transatlantic reputation was assured, not only though Anglo-American 'family' ties, identified by the GWR in the imagery of "the Brethren of the Mystic Tie" but practically through "the princely munificence of the late Mr Cecil Rhodes whose well-endowed scholarships are now bringing many more earnest students from the United States."

Of the various guides presented by the GWR, Douglas Woodruff's 'Oxford', published in 1938, was the company's fullest work on the city offering a detailed account of the historical and cultural character of the city, which, as this summary indicates, was always considered by the GWR to be of immense importance, both nationally and internationally. Woodruff's work, however, was also interesting for its recognition of a threefold identity for the city as "the home of the premier University, as one of the most rapidly growing modern towns, and as a great industrial centre and the home of the motor car now as widely known as the University itself." The GWR's theme of reconciling past with present was thus identified. Moreover, in incorporating modern industrial perspectives the GWR was emphasising its services to manufacturing interests, particularly those of a dynamic, contemporary character as in the motor trade and its ancillaries at Oxford. The company's freight services and industrial-commercial initiatives were publicised in the 1932 and 1936 editions of 'The Best Location' highlighting its amenities for the "new industries" developing in Southern, South-Eastern England.

As a powerful expression of Englishness in various forms Oxford was, thematically, an ideal south-eastern gateway to the Cotswolds. The GWR's emphasis upon the historical and cultural properties of landscape were fully exploited in its intensive celebration of rural-traditional England, as exemplified in the Cotswolds and as presented through the near reverential character of the literary work.

Below: **Oxford station, interior, circa 1910.** Although posed for and over exposed, this picture has some details of the social setting of the time. The newspaper stall lasted until recent years on many stations. Note the GWR clock.
Lens of Sutton

Above: **Leaving Oxford, 1959.** Leaving platform 1 is 4-6-0 No.5983 *Henley Hall* with an up express in the summer. The right hand arm in the off position and the lower indicator showing the number '4' tell the driver that his route was onto the main line. *Author's collection*

Below: An up express has just left platform 1 and a few moments ago the left hand signal arm returned to this position and the indicator displaying 'MAIN' would have reset to a blank screen. *Author's collection*

Above: **Interior view, circa 1930.** Looking north from the up platform shows the track layout well. There were two main line platform faces. Each platform line was linked to the corresponding main line by a scissors crossover, effectively creating four short platforms. With the removal of the roof in 1890/1, the up platform was extended north by 110 yards enlarging the bay facility for terminating services. The down platform was enlarged in 1907/8 by additions at both ends. Both up and down platforms were slightly over 300 yards long: the crossovers enabled an engine and five coaches in each half as illustrated here at the north end of the down platform. The massive bracket signals controlled the crossovers, there were miniature signals under the canopy to communicate with staff who would not be able to see the large signals when a train occupied the platform. As can be seen, circular shunting discs controlled movements the 'wrong' way, i.e. down on the up line. Next to the station clock was an exit, from the down platform to the west. The nameboard proclaims 'Junction for Worcester & West Midland, Witney, Thame, Aylesbury & Wycombe Lines'. Gas lights were the order of the day until demolition in the 1970s. One of the problems in operating the station today is that the removal of the crossovers in 1959 has resulted in only one train being able to occupy a platform at a time, hence even 3-car trains are held up outside the station while an equally small train disposes of its passengers and then moves off. *Stations UK*

Below: **Up through train, 1954.** Heading south on the main line is a train with no headcode, probably a transfer freight between the North End and South End yards. 'Dukedog' class 4-4-0 No.9015 is in charge, shed 81F was Oxford. While the signals to control the scissors crossover on the down side were by the pointwork, on the up side they were at the northern end of the platform. *R J Buckley, Initial Photographics*

Engine exchanges at Oxford. While stopping trains were allowed 2-3 minutes to do their business, Oxford was also the place where engine change-overs took place. As the down platform was adjacent to the running shed, these took 6-8 minutes; those further away and across the running lines on the up side took slightly longer. Apart from GWR locos, Oxford played host to engines from the other members of the 'Big Four' namely, LMSR, LNER and SR. It was approximately the right place, with sufficient facilities, for engines to work 'away' and 'home' in one day. The shift during 1962 of the Manchester to Bournemouth 'Pines Express', away from its Midland and Somerset & Dorset route from Birmingham to here, added a named train that needed to change engines. Southern engines had been doing this for many years with trains to / from the south coast.

Above: **Oxford, 22 August 1959.** Having arrived from the north, GWR 'Castle' class 4-6-0 No.5071 *Spitfire* will be detached from the coaches allowing SR 'Lord Nelson' class 4-6-0 No.30853 *Sir Richard Grenville*, which waits on the up through line, to take over for the remainder of the journey to Bournemouth. Bulleid 'Pacifics' and 'King Arthur' class engines were also employed on such services. *N L Browne, Ken Rogers collection*

Below: **Oxford, 1949.** The proximity of the adjacent LNWR may lead readers to believe that its engines were commonplace in the GWR station. However, as the only real link between the two rivals was through exchange sidings, this was not the case. In 1942, as part of the wartime improvements, a double junction connection was installed between the lines and henceforth, LNWR engines, especially freight locos, were often seen in the GWR station. Here class G2a 0-8-0 No.49289 is signalled off the up main at the up end of the station. *R K Blencowe collection*

Above: **Oxford, mid 1950s.** The construction of a link to the Great Central Railway's London extension, north of Banbury in 1905, brought trains from Newcastle and Sheffield hauled by GCR engines and later by LNER locos. Ready to depart north is Class B1 4-6-0 No.61092. Due to their axle loadings, GWR 'Kings' were banned from Oxford, however LNER 'V2's were used on trains to Sheffield, despite their loading being only a ¹/₂ ton different. Other LNER classes seen at Oxford included B12, D16 and K3. *R K Blencowe collection*

Below: **Oxford, 1932.** Having just arrived from the north is GWR 'Star' No.2935 *Caynham Court* with a Wolverhampton to Weymouth train – soon it will be uncoupled and replaced by an SR engine. Until 1910, when the 'Direct Line' to Birmingham opened, expresses for that city, and Wolverhampton, were routed through Oxford. One of the many interesting engine allocations to Oxford's shed was that of the three De Glenn compound 4-4-2 engines bought from France in the early 1900s. From 1915 they worked expresses to Paddington and Birmingham, all three were allocated here when withdrawn in 1926-8. *Author's collection*

Above: **Oxford down side bay, 1935.** GWR 'Metro Tank' 2-4-0T No.3585 waits with the 4.22 pm to Fairford. This bay was about 440 feet long and is host to six clerestory coaches, of which several are stored.

W Potter, Kidderminster Railway Museum

Below: **Oxford up platform, circa 1950s.** The presence of bays at its northern end allows great flexibility of service, especially for branch trains e.g. to Witney or to Blenheim. However, no such facilities exist at the southern end and so branch trains, e.g. to Princes Risborough or to Didcot, had to occupy the main platforms. This seriously affected the smooth running of the station, unless two trains could both fit in the platform. It is still the same today with main line trains queuing up north of the station while a local train occupies the single up platform. The presence of crossovers from 1908 enabled multiple occupation; however, trains started to become longer, negating their effectiveness. A single auto coach train, pushed by an 0-4-2T, with the driver in the front compartment of the trailer is at the up platform.

Author's collection

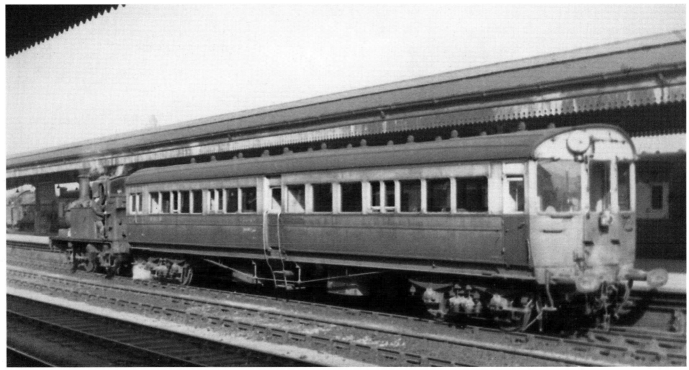

Above: **Oxford Station North, 6 October 1958**. 'Modified Hall' 4-6-0 No.6976 *Graythwaite Hall* coasts into the up platform with an express. The tracks are passing over the connection between the Oxford Canal and the River Thames: Sheepwash Channel. The controlling signal box is on the right. The wooden engine shed is over on the left of the running lines. The white indicator boxes below the arms informed the driver which line he was to go to. On the left are two large wooden bracket signals, they were replaced by one signal gantry in November the next year, as seen below.

RAS Marketing

Below: **Oxford Station North, 1962**. Emerging under the impressive signal gantry is 2800 class 2-8-0 No.2836, almost sixty years old. The World War Two protection against bomb blasts is evident in the brick lower part of the 100 lever signal box,originally of 1899 vintage. The gantry, with associated connections, took twelve days to build in November 1959.

Author's collection

19

Oxford engine shed. When the GWR extended the broad gauge line from Millstream Junction north to Banbury, they built, like most things at Oxford, a two road wooden shed just north of the up platform, complete with a turntable between the shed and the station, just before the Channel. Meanwhile, the 'narrow' gauge OWW had built a single road, again wooden, shed north of the Channel, on the down side in Cripley Meadow, probably in the mid 1850s, it also having a turntable. With the reduction in broad gauge services from the early 1860s, the GWR's shed became less used and when those services ceased in the area from 1872, the shed was converted for use by carriages. It was demolished in 1879. The single track OWW shed became increasingly overstretched in the mid 1860s and so the GWR, prior to its takeover of the West Midland Railway, into which the OWW had grown, built a four road shed in 1862, incorporating the original OWW shed, and remodelled the site including installing a larger turntable. Incidentally, the LNWR shed at Rewley Road closed in 1950 with the transfer of their engines here, this presented some problems as the vacuum brake system on the ex-LNWR 'Super' D 0-8-0 engines was different to that of the GWR. The shed officially closed to steam from 3 January 1966.

Below: At the coaling stage is 1400 class 0-4-2T No.1437 in 1957. The brick shed was a wartime improvement, but the method of operation was distinctly antediluvian – it involved lots of manpower. The original coaling stage, made of wood and corrugated iron, was on a dead end line situated near to the access road, which caused congestion. Oxford's allocation in the early 1940s was governed by the fact that only engines with smaller tenders could pass under the coaling ramp. This restriction on operations was removed by the construction of this double sided building in 1944 and its resiting and remodelling of track, close to the turntable. Imagine how many of these skips would have to be tipped into, say, a tender holding eight tons of coal, that amount would have been shovelled into the skips from wagons in the middle of the coaling stage by hand.   *L G Marshall, R K Blencowe collection*

Left, above: Arriving on shed in August 1954 is Class D16/3 4-4-0 No.62585. On the right is railcar W4. To the right of it were the repair shops. Extension of the north end of the down station platform in 1908 resulted in the end of the shed nearest the running lines being shortened by approximately fifty feet to accommodate the new access track; the opportunity to refurbish the shed was taken at that time too. The wartime remodelling sorted the access problem out by allowing entry to be from the north, opposite the new Oxford North Junction, and exit from the south, adjacent to the shed. In April 1960 the shed was reroofed.   *Rail Archive Stephenson*

Above: An essential feature at all major engine sheds was the turntable, occupied here by 'Bulldog' class 4-4-0 No.3454 *Skylark* in 1951. The siting of such an important part of shed routine is critical to the smooth running of the depot; at Oxford it has been in three different places! In 1944, under the wartime Transport Finance Act, Oxford North yard and the locomotive yard were further remodelled. An unmanned engine, No.48417, at the adjacent coaling stage, put it out of action for just over a month in September 1957 by falling into the turntable pit! During that time, engines went 'in convoy' to Yarnton to turn on its triangle of lines or the turntable there.

Brian Moone, Kidderminster Railway Museum

Below: **Oxford North Yard, 21 April 1934**. Waiting in the sidings that make up Oxford North Yard is 4-4-0 No.3279 *Torbay*. Rumour has it that passengers thought that the nameplates on engines of the 'Badminton' class were train destinations causing confusion and leading to removal from that class by May 1927. This yard closed in 1942 when Hinksey came into operation. The rings on signal arms, indicating goods lines, were dispensed with from November 1949.   *H F Wheeller collection*

Above: **The LNWR at Oxford**. Arriving from Bletchley in the north, the company built a terminus at Rewley Road, adjacent to which the GWR was building its through station. Opening on 20 May 1851 it pre-dated the GWR station and its style was outwardly similar to that at Banbury, Merton Street. The facilities for passengers consisted of an island platform with a transverse ridge & furrow glazed roof. At the buffer stop end were the booking office and other facilities.

The OWW used the goods yard here as it was faced with adding narrow gauge lines to reach the GWR's broad gauge goods depot situated up from Millstream Junction at the old passenger station. So the OWW, having been supported financially and in other ways, bit the hand that fed it and sent its freight to the GWR's rival. Suffice to say that the GWR was less than pleased, souring forever the relationship with the OWW.

After the construction of Oxford North Junction as part of wartime improvements, passenger services were switched to the bay platforms at the GWR station from 1951. *Lens of Sutton*

Right, above: **Leaving Oxford, 1960**. Having been given the right away to proceed from the down platform onto the down main, 'Hall' class 4-6-0 No.5918 *Walton Hall* passes over the complex pointwork leading to the engine shed on the right. *RAS Marketing*

The allocation at OXF Oxford in June 1947			
4-6-0	15	2-4-0T	4
2-8-0	9	0-6-0T	15
2-6-0	4	0-6-2T	2
0-6-0	2	0-4-2T	3
2-6-2T	3	Diesel Railcar	2
		Total	**59**

At the end of the 1950s, almost 180 passenger and freight trains a day used the restricted facilities at Oxford. Add to this a large number of trip workings augmented by the various engine exchanges, and it will be clear that Oxford was a very busy station indeed!

Below: **Oxford North Junction**. This fine panorama shows the facilities as they were from the mid 1940s. The LNWR lines are on the left with 'Hall' class 4-6-0 No.4948 *Northwick Hall* on its way north. The GWR's main lines are to the right. The four tracks are paired by direction with the fast lines in the middle. Making up the background are the carriage sidings with the line through the brick coaling stage showing up well. North Yard is off to the extreme right. Up goods trains waiting their slot through the station had the opportunity to refill their tender tanks from the water column, slightly in front of the controlling signal post, complete with miniature bracket. The double junctions between the rival company's lines was completed in October 1942, the controlling signal box, hidden by the train's coaches and dwarfed by the water tower next to it, was a GWR 'ARP' style, similar to those at Hinksey. It was completely of brick with concrete floors and roof, as already mentioned built to survive a bomb blast. At the time of nationalisation, the GWR alone had lower quadrant signals and, as part of an experiment, a pair of upper quadrant signals replaced the up main starter signals here sometime in 1950. Simply the GWR spectacle plate was turned upside down and the rod to the arm pushed it to the 'off' position. In 1973 the signals were removed, with no apparent evaluation of this experiment, and are now in the National Railway Museum. A similar signal was erected at Portishead. *Author's collection*

EXTRACT FROM GWR SERVICE TIME TABLE DATED OCTOBER 1879

Trains from Oxford for OWW line

Weekday Trains		Depart Oxford
Oxford, Yarnton and Aberdare empties	RR W	12.40am
London and Worcester goods		1.20am
Oxford, Yarnton and Aberdare coal	W	1.40am
London, Worcester, Dudley, Wolverhampton and South Wales goods		3.5am
Oxford, Yarnton and Aberdare empties	MX	3.45am
Witney and East Gloucester goods	MX	6.10am
Oxford-Aberdare coal empties		6.40am
London and Worcester goods	MX	7.0am
Oxford Worcester and Wolverhampton local goods		7.30am
Oxford-West Midland passenger		8.15am
Oxford-Witney passenger		8.50am
Oxford-West Midland passenger		11.50am
Oxford-Witney passenger		12.5pm
West Midland coal empties	RR	12.15pm
Oxford Fairford and Witney goods		2.0pm
London-West Midland passenger		4.10pm
Oxford-West Midland passenger		4.20pm
Oxford-Witney passenger		4.35pm
Oxford-Wolverhampton goods		7.50pm
Oxford-West Midland passenger		8.17pm
Oxford-Witney passenger		8.45pm
Oxford, Yarnton and Aberdare coal empties		9.40pm

RR Runs as required
MX Except Mondays
W Departs Wolvercot Siding

EXTRACT FROM GWR SERVICE TIME TABLE DATED OCTOBER 1879

Trains into Oxford from OWW line

Weekday Trains		Arrive Oxford
Wolverhampton. Dudley, Worcester and London goods and minerals		12.00am
Aberdare and Yarnton coal train	MX	1.55am
Worcester and London goods	MX	2.50am
Wolverhampton and Didcot goods	MX	4.55am
West Midland local goods	MX	6.55am
Aberdare and Yarnton coal train	MX	7.50am
Witney-Oxford passenger		8.30am
West Midland-Oxford passenger		8.50am
Aberdare and Yarnton coal train		9.10am
West Midland-Oxford coal train	RR	11.5am
Witney-Oxford passenger		11.25am
West Midland-Oxford passenger		11.50am
Pontypool and Yarnton coal	RR MX	12.15pm
Fairford and Witney goods		1.25pm
West Midland-Oxford passenger		1.45pm
Aberdare and Yarnton coal		2.15pm
Witney-Oxford passenger		3.50pm
West Midland-London passenger		4.25pm
Witney-Oxford passenger		7.45pm
Worcester, Oxford and London goods		8.20pm
Witney-Oxford goods		8.30pm
West Midland-Oxford passenger		8.50pm

RR Runs as required
MX Except Mondays
W Departs Wolvercot Siding

Above: **North of Oxford, 15 October 1962.** There were quadruple lines for about three miles beyond the station to Wolvercot Junction. Passing with express freight headcode is an oil train, probably from Rowley Regis, near Stourbridge, on its way to Fawley, near Southampton. Hauling it is 2800 class 2-8-0 No.2898. *R K Blencowe collection*

Below: **Wolvercot siding, 10 April 1953.** Approaching Oxford is 4-6-0 No.5032 Usk Castle at the head of an express from Worcester. The down goods loop is the other side of the ditch to the left and the up goods line is the track to the right of the train. In the background is the LNWR's Port Meadow signal box and carriage sidings. The footpath crossing the lines here was the spur for that company to build a halt in 1905 as part of its rail motor services from Oxford to Bicester. During wartime improvements it was swept away and sidings added instead.

R K Blencowe collection

Above: **Port Meadow, 1930s**. LNER 'Atlantic' 4-4-2 No.3276 has just left Oxford with its train of GWR coaches. Its route to Sheffield will involve Banbury and then turning onto ex-GCR lines heading for Rugby, Leicester and Nottingham.   *Milepost 92½ Picture collection*

Below: **Wolvercot, 13 June 1914**. GWR steam railcar No.74 nears the halt at Wolvercot with the 2.50pm from Blenheim to Oxford. Such trains were introduced for several services in the area including to Princes Risborough, Heyford and Shipton from 1908. It necessitated the construction of wooden platforms at places like Hinksey and here at Wolvercot. The services stopped in the Great War. The LNWR introduced a similar concept on their line to Bletchley, also with a halt at Wolvercote. Behind the coach is a wagon that was built to carry gas for the railway's use. No. 74 was built at Swindon in 1906 with the body constructed by Gloucester Carriage & Wagon Co. After a useful life the engine was removed from the coach in 1928, the latter becoming trailer No.203 in1933. *Ken Nunn collection / LCGB*

Above: **Wolvercot Junction, early 1960s.** Having joined the line from Banbury, the engine driver will want to speed up from the 40mph restriction imposed over the junction. In charge of the up 'Cathedrals Express' is No.7034 *Ince Castle*. This is the start of quadruple track all the way through Oxford station and south to Hinksey yard. Wolvercot signal box was down to the left with the signalman having pulled lever No.5 to drop the arm on the bracket signal in the rear showing that the driver was to take the up main line south. This view was taken from the A40 overbridge.

David Lawrence, Hugh Davies collection

Right: Railway Clearing House diagram from around 1914. The LNWR route to Bletchley and connecting curve at Yarnton invade the GWR scene. Prior to the GWR takeover in 1864 of the West Midland Railway (WMR) – formed in 1860 and which incorporated the OWW, Worcester & Hereford and Newport, Abergavenny and Hereford – virtually all the WMR's London traffic was travelling over the curve to and from Bletchley. This meant the GWR was losing out on a lot of business, so gathering the WMR into its fold was a very important move.

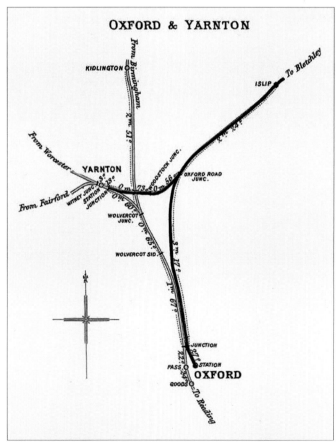

OXFORD & YARNTON

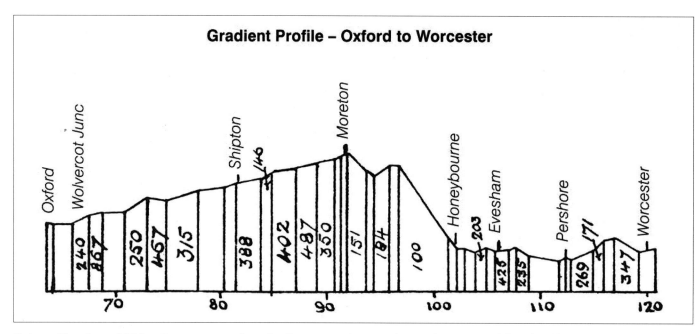

Gradient Profile – Oxford to Worcester

Below: **Yarnton, 1930s.** Some years after the line started operations, the West Midland Railway opened a station here on 14 November 1861, along with the branch to Witney; it just saw its centenary, closing on 18 June 1962. The photographer was standing in the down line, looking towards Oxford. Note the fancy roof of the shelter. The lower signal on the up line is for the LNWR route to Bletchley. The signal box is perched high up so as to allow the signalman a clear view of the line, perhaps it was the LNWR's preferred type of box at the time of building the connection. Iron ore trains came from Irthlingborough, beyond Northampton, to South Wales and used this route to get to Honeybourne and then to Cheltenham. Bristol was an important port for the importation of petrol, as well as some South Wales ports. During the Second World War as many as ten trains a day of petrol and general goods were diverted from the main line to London via such places as Yarnton, presumably to reduce the chances of being bombed.

Stations UK

Above: **Yarnton, 1934.** The LNWR built a connection of just over one and a half miles, seen veering off left, to its Buckinghamshire Railway, which went to Bletchley; it opened on 1 April 1854. It also made a link so that trains could run direct to Rewley Road, Oxford. In later years Wolvercote Halt was built on the link. By means of these lines the LNWR ran Euston to Worcester trains with connections to Oxford in earlier times. *Mowat collection*

Below: **Yarnton, 1934.** Yarnton was actually a station sandwiched between two junctions. Looking towards Worcester shows the platforms well but obscures some of the signals. At the end of the down platform, in the middle of the picture, the line to Witney and Fairford branches off. The house on the up platform was built by the OWW for its station staff as was the vogue at the time – almost on top of the line. It also housed the booking office and waiting rooms. Trains from Fairford looked as if they were to going to crash into it until at the last moment, when the train swung to the right on joining the main line. The house was demolished around 1935. Note the ornate gents urinals, on the up side. *Mowat collection*

Branch to Witney and Fairford

Left, above: **Witney, late 1950s.** A traveller by train on the opening day, 14 November 1861, would have alighted at a terminus station a few hundred yards north of this point. This was the end of the twelve miles-long Witney Railway which delivered wool and transported the finished products, blankets, from the town, worked by the West Midland Railway. Soon after opening, plans were drawn up to extend the line to Cheltenham and connect with a branch from the GWR main line at Faringdon by the East Gloucestershire Railway. However, only a fourteen mile extension to Fairford was ever built, opening on 15 January 1873. The terminus at Witney was made into a goods station with a new through station being built a short distance to the south. Almost half of the 100,000 tons of freight carried along the line in 1929 was for Witney. The line also carried 120,000 passengers that year too. This view is towards Oxford from the diverted Station Road bridge. There was a small wooden shelter on the other platform as well as a water column, both just hidden by the tree on the right. *Joe Moss collection*

Left, below: **Brize Norton & Bampton, 1961.** In common with much of rural Britain, the agricultural area around here experienced depopulation in the latter part of the nineteenth century, the railway doing little to stimulate industry. For most of its existence the line saw minor alterations, but the biggest upheavals came prior to the Second World War when the airfield to the north was built in 1936-38. The station was called Bampton (Oxon) until May 1940 when the GWR decided that a town of the same name in Devon was causing confusion. Pannier tank No.4649 waits with a train for Oxford. *E T Gill, R K Blencowe collection*

Above: **Fairford, 12 August 1953.** With the extension of the line, a new terminus was built here, and is viewed from an overbridge. The signal box is almost at the end of the single platform, beyond is a typical stone goods shed, and in the background is the small engine shed and parachute water tank. About to set off with the 2.10 pm for Oxford is 7400 class 0-6-0PT No.7411. The signalling is interesting – there is a home signal to control progress along the line towards the engine shed. In front of the train the lower, distant, arm is 'fixed'. When the GWR thought about Automatic Train Control from 1906, they used this branch for the experiments. The branch was proposed in 1923 to be extended to Cirencester to meet the Cheltenham to Andover line, ex Midland & South Western Junction Railway. A cost estimate for the eight miles line was £321,000. The rationale for the line was that construction would reduce unemployment: it was, along with others, vetoed, as the Government was keen to see permanent, not temporary, employment resulting from its loans. *R K Blencowe collection*

Above: **Handborough, 1954.** The OWW opened this station on 4 June 1854 and, due to its proximity to the birthplace of the Churchill family, the company added 'for Blenheim'. on the name boards. Of course there was a branch to that village from the main Banbury line but to get there, passengers would have to go almost eight miles into Oxford, change trains for Kidlington, and then, perhaps, change again for Blenheim. In later days a few trains made the nine mile through trip from Oxford. Looking towards Oxford shows the primitive conditions on the down platform with passengers having to cross the line for Worcester trains. This station was quite busy, as both platforms were extended at the up ends thirty years after opening. On the left is the up refuge siding with its opposite number being on the right of the picture. The siding on the left served a loading dock, the tall building in the background is the goods shed, accessed by trailing connections from up and down lines. The signal box is barely visible at the eastern end of the down platform and there were two sidings just beyond it on the down side. During the Second World War the Ministry of Food added a loop into Beck's sidings where there was a loading facility. These were accessed by an extension of the line from the goods shed. Trains still stop here, but only the up line has been used since 29 November 1971 – and the station is now called Hanborough...

Stations UK

32

Above: Handborough, 19 October 1957. Looking north-west towards Worcester shows the road bridge from which the previous picture was taken. A new shelter has been built on the down platform. Hauling a fitted freight towards Oxford is 2-8-0 No.2899. When the line opened, this was the first station and consequently, when the LNWR ran their trains from Bletchley to the area, it was here that they called with passengers changing for Oxford: 'Handborough Junction'. This situation persisted until Yarnton Junction opened in 1861. Much of the down platform still remains, albeit a wonderful place to cultivate primroses!

R M Casserley

Above: **Combe Halt, 31 August 1952**. Passengers from Worcester would alight on this platform. Although only a mile from Handborough the GWR was attempting to fight bus – and car – competition by opening the halt, which had staggered platforms, on 8 July 1935. The sleeper-made platform would be too uneven to pass today's standards. Note the 'Tilley' lamp on the concrete post. Although a halt is still open here, a new platform – which must be one of the rail network's shortest – was built with the singling of the line in the early 1970s. *T C Cole*

Below: **North of Combe, 31 August 1952**. An Oxford bound express hauled by No.5092 *Tresco Abbey* prepares to pass Combe Halt. The siding on the left which led to a saw mill, was removed three years after this picture was taken. One over-riding feature of the area that the line passes through is a slow but steady rural depopulation. The line, though certainly bringing goods to the area, failed to stimulate growth, except for localised, small, domestic industries. *T C Cole*

Above: **Finstock Halt, 18 July 1959**. Approximately half a mile before arriving at Finstock from Oxford the line crosses the River Evenlode, for the seventh time. Adjacent to this was a connection to the Fawler Iron & Coal Co, which extracted iron ore, using a tramway in the mid 1880s for a few short years until collapse of the mine's roof. Looking towards Oxford shows respectable facilities, by today's standards – twin corrugated iron shelters, accessed from the B4022. In response to the growing threat of the motor car the GWR opened the halt on 9 April 1934. According to BR, it closed on 5 May 1969. Although it reopened, from 9 March 1987, the old up platform ceased to be used and a new one was built on the down side. The single line has been slewed to pass under the tallest part of the bridge, the platform being correspondingly extended. *H C Casserley*

Below: **Charlbury. 18 July 1959**. This was one of the original stations that opened with the line on 4 June 1853, and is still in business. The area use to be well-known for glove making. The track layout for the station, and its services, is very similar to Handborough: here there was an extended siding to the north of the wooden goods shed. As there was no trailing slip when crossing the up line, shunting operations necessitated blockage of both lines. The line as far as Moreton-in-Marsh follows the river valley. This may keep gradients moderate, but increases the mileage, removes the line from centres of population and the number of river crossings (at least 10) adds to construction costs. *H C Casserley*

Left, above: **Charlbury, 1967**. Looking towards Worcester shows the expected patronage was mostly for Oxford, however it was the Worcester platform that was extended in 1928 towards the road bridge. There are two alternatives to hoisting signals high up in the air to make them stand out, and both were tried here. One was to make the signal post shorter and visible through the arches of the bridge, which was the situation here until the early 1960s with the down starter being on the 'wrong' side too. One disadvantage is that it may be obscured by a passing train. The other was painting the background, as here where the down starter shows up well against the brickwork. Notice the GWR water tank behind the down shelter. *Stations UK*

Left, below: **Charlbury, 18 July 1959**. The station buildings on the up platform are the original, built for the OWW in 1853. This single storey wooden building is almost 33' long by over 12' wide. To begin with it had a booking hall, waiting room, ladies toilet and a ticket office. Strangely, male urinals were not originally provided although, as can be seen, the GWR added them by punching a hole in the side wall and putting a matching wooden screen around the entrance. The seats are GWR too. While the chimney top is not original it does illustrate that, with some effort, our railway heritage can be preserved and still carry out its original function if it is looked after. The style of roof was used elsewhere (Yatton, Aldermaston and Mortimer) even if their buildings were brick. Note the arches over the doors and windows, it would have been so easy to make them flat but some effort has been made to produce a pleasing effect. The River Evenlode is crossed, just out of sight, around the curve towards Oxford. *H C Casserley*

Above: **Charlbury troughs**. Even though express trains stopped at Oxford and Worcester and the distance between them is not great, 57 1/2 miles, the GWR built water troughs mid-way between Charlbury and Ascott in 1906. This enabled trains to spend a shorter time in the main stations so allowing a speeding up of the service, also reducing congestion at Oxford and Worcester which both have only one up and one down through platform. South of Charlbury station, on the down side, was a siding serving a small pumping house for the troughs, presumably with water from the adjacent, and ever present, River Evenlode. Although the troughs were 560 yards long, travelling at a modest 60mph means that there are less than 20 seconds to perform all the manoeuvres necessary. If the fireman misjudges things then the tender tanks overflow, soaking everyone, including passengers in the first few compartments of the 1.10pm Worcester to Paddington, if the windows were open. The troughs needed extensive maintenance in 1952, hampering their function and so reducing the timekeeping of up expresses at Oxford. *Paul Riley, The Restoration & Archiving Trust*

Above: **Ascott-under-Wychwood, 26 April 1962.** When the OWW opened this station on 4 June 1853 it was simply Ascott, the GWR added the rest of the name on 1 February 1880. The main buildings were on the Worcester platform, perhaps owing more to the road layout than the number of passengers expected. It is at this platform that trains have stopped since 1971, although the single line is mainly slewed over to the former up trackbed. Compared to other stations on the line, more passengers were expected than at Charlbury and Handborough as the buildings were larger, but not as many as Evesham, which had bigger ones still, and built of brick! Much of the geology of the area is what is called stonebrash. This is excellent land for sheep and barley, however the presence of the weed charlock which, until the use of chemical fertilisers in the 1950s, needed hand weeding, was a serious drawback.

P J Garland collection

Below: **Ascott-under-Wychwood, 18 July 1959.** The disparity between patronage is very marked at Ascott as Oxford bound passengers had a simple wooded shelter. Freight facilities consisted of a loop on the down side accessed by trailing connections to both lines. There were single sidings from each end of the loop. On 24 May 1965 BR decided that Ascott should be a halt, but reverted to its former status nearly four years later on 5 May 1969. East of the station there is a speed restriction notice for drivers – 100mph maximum! West of the station the line becomes double for the just over eleven miles to Moreton-in-Marsh.

H C Casserley

Above: **Shipton 'for Burford', 1951.** Shipton is just over a mile and a quarter from Ascott towards Worcester. Like Ascott, the station opened with the line, is still open, and had 'Halt' status for a few years in the mid-1960s, from 3 January 1966 until 5 May 1969. Burford is five miles to the south, and Chipping Norton six to the north. A typical three coach stopping train is heading for Oxford. Like Charlbury, the Worcester bound platforms were longer than the up ones. The goods facility to the east of the station was a long loading dock while on the down side was a siding where wagons are stabled. The signal box dates from 1884. The large building on the left is Matthews flour depot.

Stations UK

Below: **Shipton, 26 April 1962.** Interestingly, the station buildings on the Oxford platform were of brick construction, augmented by the typical GWR corrugated iron store, complete with a sack truck – like in a scene on a model railway. The down starter signal is to the left and in the distance, below the arm for the advance starter, is a smaller arm. This has an 'S' on it being used for shunting movements to the goods shed accessed by a trailing crossover. Wooden boards allow walking across the point rodding in the foreground which ends up at the signal box, just off to the left.

P J Garland collection

Below: **Kingham, 13 June 1953.** With the time around ten past five, two trains prepare to depart at 5.15pm. On the right, at platform 2, is a stopping train for Oxford, the driver passing the time of day with one of the station staff. Omitting the Yarnton stop, the train would arrive at 6pm. Oxford shed, 81F, was 'home' for 2-6-2T No.4147. At platform 1, on the left, is a train for Cheltenham, hauled by the smaller variety of 2-6-2T, a member of the 4500 class. This would have also worked the 4pm service to Chipping Norton and back. Usually, Cheltenham trains arrived at the island platform, the engine would be uncoupled and run-round the coaches, and so be ready to haul them back to Cheltenham. The Chipping Norton service was partly diesel rail car operated in the early 1950s. Note that the typical GWR water crane has an extended arm, under it is a brazier to prevent it freezing in cold weather. *T J Edgington*

Left, above: **Kingham, 1931**. The OWW opened a station here on 10 August 1855, after the main line had been running for two years, as Chipping Norton Junction. The villages of Kingham (half a mile to the north-east, population around 625 at the line's opening) or Bledington (half a mile to the west) could have been alternative names, however the dominant town of the area was Chipping Norton (population just under 3,000), hence the name. In spite of being the junction for Bourton as well as Chipping Norton from 1862, it was not until 1 May 1909 that the station name changed to Kingham. Looking north shows the face of the original island platform that Chipping Norton trains ('The Chippy Nippy' or the 'Chippy Dick') used when the branch was open. A simple loop enabled engines to be released to run round the coaches for the return journey. At the far end of the platform there was a single connection to the sidings north of the station. Although the opening of the branch west to Bourton-on-the-Water include modification of the existing sidings, it was the extension from there to Cheltenham that precipitated the remodelling of the lines and the extension of the station in 1883. Platform 4, on the right, complete with a small shelter, was built for trains arriving from Banbury. The footbridge, with GWR logo, offered a safe crossing of two sets of running lines. On the extreme right can be seen the small addition to the bridge allowing access to the Langstone Hotel. The space underneath the stairs to the island platform, was developed as a refreshment room in the 1930s. As only about 30-35 passengers a day booked from Kingham, with 45-50 season tickets, it must have relied heavily upon passengers waiting for connecting services. After the venture closed, the space became a bicycle store. In the hundred years after the line opened, the population of Kingham remained static: Chipping Norton's more than doubled.

Author's collection

Above: **Kingham, 18 July 1959**. Platform, No.1, on the right, is the down main at which trains from Oxford stop. The 1883 buildings are still imposing in yellow brick with red and black string courses, they replaced the earlier wooden ones. To cope with the extra demands of the two branches from here to Chipping Norton and Bourton-on-the-Water after their extensions to Banbury and Cheltenham respectively, the track layout at the north end of the station was modified in the early 1880s. The island platform was extended, by about 115', the change in levels can be seen, and the signal box that was there initially was rebuilt a short distance north along the main line. Under the bridge was the south junction. Here, from 1884, the branch from Banbury was connected to the main line. In 1906 the GWR started a 1.40pm Paddington to Worcester non-stop train. As it approached here, it slipped a coach which was attached to the 3.20pm train to Cheltenham, arriving there at 4.12pm; in the time table the train was advertised as the 'Cheltenham, Worcester, Malvern & Hereford Express'. The coach was sent back to the capital by being attached to the 11.25am ex-Worcester when it stopped here. The slip coach workings were suspended during the Great War and afterwards lasted until 1926. Passengers from Chipping Norton, by changing here and having a long wait, had connections to the capital, although they could also go via Banbury until 1951.

R M Casserley

Above: **Kingham engine shed, 30 May 1958**. A single track shed was opened in 1881, and in 1884 its access was from the Banbury line. In 1906 it was deemed too small and was closed. The replacement Churchward-style shed, large enough for two tank engines, was authorised in 1912 at an estimated cost of £1,343, but would make a saving of £1,210 per annum. It had been considered earlier, in 1906, but a decision delayed until the effects of the direct line could be evaluated. To the right of the attendant engine, BR Standard 2-6-0 No.78009, was a turntable and to its left was a standard GWR water tank. This engine, allocated to 85A, Worcester, worked the freight service to Chipping Norton for some time. It stabled at the shed overnight. Earlier in the 1950s, a Collett 0-6-0 from Gloucester shed also stayed here overnight. The shed's roof had seen better times, in 1962 the shed closed completely. *R M Casserley*

Branches to Cheltenham and Banbury

Both to the east and west of the main line, branches were built and later extended to link up with other parts of the GWR system providing a valuable cross-country route. The Cheltenham line lasted as a through one until October 1962, when the passenger service came off, though freight continued from Kingham to Bourton until 1964. Kingham -Banbury passenger trains were cut back to Chipping Norton in 1951, being withdrawn completely in October 1962. The journey from Kingham to Cheltenham took an hour: no wonder the GWR developed a bus service from Cheltenham to Oxford in 1928, taking away potential passengers from the Kingham branch. The switch back up and down at 1 in 60 near Andoversford, the gradients at Stow and the similar nature of the line beyond Chipping Norton often necessitated doubleheading of iron ore trains on the branches.

West to Cheltenham

Right, above: **Stow-on-the-Wold, 29 July 1956**. Gradients of 1 in 83 face trains from both directions, while the village the station serves is about 200' above the line, illustrating the hilly terrain on the fringe of the Cotswolds. The station was also a goodly walk away from Stow! Most of the line was single. Here 4500 Class 2-6-2T No.5514 is just about to enter the station. There was a long loading bank serviced by two loops. The Cheltenham-Kingham passenger service in BR days amounted to six trains each way Monday to Saturday, but no Sunday service. *Gregory*

Right, below: **Bourton-on-the Water, June 1960**. Following a Bill for the Bourton-on-the-Water Railway in 1859, the OWW's successor, The West Midland Railway, undertook to work and maintain the branch, which opened from Chipping Norton Junction on 1 March 1862. Passenger services were delayed until September of the next year as the stations were not ready. Plans existed for, but were not acted upon, for a west to north curve at Chipping Norton Junction so that trains from Honeybourne could proceed onto the branch without a reversal. Bourton was the terminus of the line for nineteen years until the GWR extended it to Cheltenham in 1881. The connection at Andoversford with the Midland & South Western Junction line to Swindon and Andover from 1891 led to the doubling of the section from there to Cheltenham in 1902. Arriving with a train from Kingham is 4500 Class 2-6-2T No.4573. The passing loop here was just over a quarter of a mile long after being extended in 1906. Note the contrasting facilities, Kingham-bound passengers had only a small shelter: both platforms have respectable patronage. The new signals, and controlling box, hidden away behind the water tank on the left, were also products of the 1906 improvements, the cabin used to be further to the east. The main station building dates from the early 1930s. To the west, the line would cross the River Windrush. *E T Gill, R K Blencowe collection*

East to Banbury

Above: **Sarsden Halt, 20 June 1940**. The OWW sponsored the short – 4 mile – extension east to Chipping Norton in 1855. While most of the line is single track, all the stations, apart from the two halts added later, had passing loops and two platform faces. Originally in 1893 a 'Drop Platform' was opened here which was upgraded to full 'Halt' status on 2 July 1906. As this picture with GWR railcar No.10 shows, a short loop and a siding also existed. The single wooden platform, complete with war-time blackout method of highlighting edges, was deemed adequate for the inhabitants of the village of Churchill, to the south. Just after nationalisation the service consisted of six train per day, each way, with four going all the way to Banbury. *Lens of Sutton collection, R Carpenter*

Below: **Chipping Norton, around 1960**. The state of the Chipping Norton Railway's finances and the potential traffic for revenue generation meant that this was the end of the line in 1855. However, north and west Oxfordshire had deposits of iron ore: South Wales and South Staffordshire had the steel making capacity. Consequently, the GWR built a line to here from King's Sutton on its main London to Birmingham route in 1887, so allowing services to be extended from Kingham to Banbury. North-east of the station is a small outcrop from the Cotswolds. This necessitated building a 685 yard tunnel through the rocks and shifting the site of the original station, which became part of the goods yard from 1909. Waiting to leave for Kingham and Cheltenham is 2-6-2T No.4573. By this date the passenger service was minimal, just one return in the morning – a mixed – and one in the afternoon. The local woollen industry made a variety of tweed called 'Bliss', named after the owner of the mill! *D Johnson collection, Millbrook House Ltd.*

Above: **Kingham avoiding line**. An important cross-country service was developed by the GWR and the GCR when, in 1906, the two branches that fed into Kingham Junction were connected by a direct, double track, line obviating the necessity to enter and reverse in the station. From the west this needed a short section of 1 in 80, and from the east the access was via a stiffer 1 in 62 gradient. While attractive for cross-country trains, the twisting nature of the line kept speeds slow, as well as a 20mph restriction over Hook Norton viaduct, so the proper potential of the route was never achieved. The through service was the 'Barry & Newcastle Express', later becoming the 'South Wales Ports, Gloucester, Leicester, Nottingham, York & Newcastle Express'. Motive power changed from 4-4-0s to 2-6-0s to brand-new 'Manor' class 4-6-0s, the latter usually being in charge between Banbury and Gloucester, until September 1939 when the outbreak of war put paid to this service on the route. In this picture a 2-6-0 brings a northbound train over the OWW main line towards Kingham East junction, with Kingham East Loop signal box on the left. *Mowat collection*

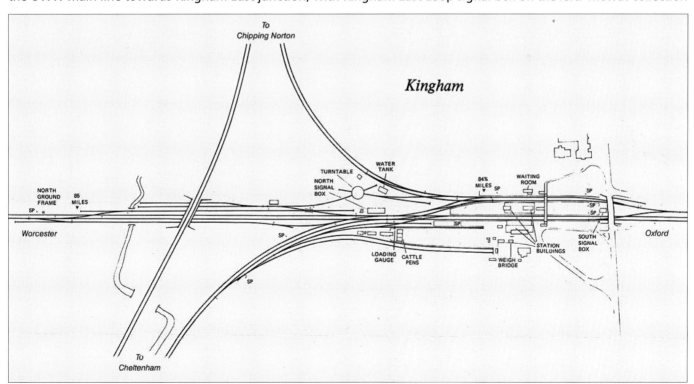

Above: **Adlestrop, after 1904, prior to the Great War**. Another station opened with the line on 4 June 1853 by the OWW as Addlestrop and Stow Road. The last part was dropped from 1 March 1862, due to the opening of the branch from Chipping Norton Junction, and one 'd' removed from the name twenty years later on 1 August 1883. This GWR official portrait shows the company's preferred way of crossing the line. The up platform from which this picture was taken has been extended to the foot of the road bridge and at the southern end of the down platform, beyond the ramp, a flat surface has been provided. Both of these areas have a series of lamps on them, and joining them is a sleeper based crossing of the lines, with suitable safety warnings. For down expresses on the inside of the curve this must have been hazardous. The up starter signal, visible under the bridge, is not well sighted and later, by 1946, was moved to the end of the up platform. The down platform was extended also, at its northern end. The bridge, now the A426, crosses the River Evenlode on the right before going to Stow, a couple of miles to the west.   *GWR, R S Carpenter collection*

Below: **Adlestrop, 1960**. Calling with a stopping train is 'Mogul' No.6349. The standard goods shed shows up well, there were loading areas both sides. The shed obscures the signal box; on the down side is the refuge siding. The station house was accessed by a footpath across the river, on the left. The wooden buildings, including the small shelter on the Worcester side, probably the original, have lost their canopies, a prelude to closure on 3 January 1966.
R K Blencowe collection

Above: **Moreton-in-Marsh.** A fine panoramic view looking towards the station and the Worcester direction. Note the replacement signal box and altered goods shed compared with the pictures on page 48.   *Author's collection*

Below: **Moreton-in-Marsh, 1949**. June 4 1853 saw the opening of a station here by the OWW. On the right is the platform for Oxford trains; a train for Worcester can be seen passing under the bridge in the distance. While the main station buildings were replaced by brick ones by the GWR in 1872, (they are still in use) the island platform still has wooden ones. To break up an otherwise plain building, string courses of different coloured bricks have been used, which, with the colour scheme of the door and the position of the poster makes quite an attractive end to the building. A large covered footbridge enabled passengers to cross the line, curiously, to give passengers continuous coverage one would have expected it to be built nearer to the main buildings and not half way down the platform. The line is now single from here to Evesham. This is the highest point on the line.   *J Moss collection, R Carpenter*

Above: **Moreton-in-Marsh, 24 April 1955**. An old horse-worked tramway to Shipston-on-Stour was reopened by the GWR from 1 July 1889. Waiting at the branch platform is a PW train hauled by 'Dean Goods' 0-6-0 No.2474, just days from withdrawal, and almost certainly the last of this venerable class to be seen here. The exchange sidings on the left were laid in the early 1880s for exchange of wagons. The branch ceased to carry passengers in 1929 and freight from 1960. Apart from the goods shed, there were three sidings at the Worcester end of the down platform. And electric lights have arrived! *R K Blencowe collection*

Below: **Moreton-in-Marsh, 1949**. From the end of the up platform a good view is achieved of the goods shed and signal box, the latter is still in use. Cattle pens are off to the right. Note the down home signal in the six foot way between up and down lines to enable it to be seen: its normal site would be obscured by the bridge and the goods shed. Note also the small shunting arm on the same post. There used to be a signal box at the other end of the platform as well, but upon extension of the island platform it closed and its functions taken over by the box in the picture. Under the bridge a down refuge siding was added. Wartime alterations converted this into a loop and a refuge siding was also built. *J Moss collection, R Carpenter*

Branch to Shipston-on-Stour

The origins of this line came from the desire for a canal to compete with the Grand Junction Canal from Birmingham to London. The Central Junction Tramway was to connect the Stratford-on-Avon Canal with the River Thames at Eynsham Wharf. The section from Stratford to Moreton opened in 1826 with horses pulling wagons on 4' gauge tracks. Ten years later a short extension to Shipston-on-Stour opened, but lack of money prevented further development – and then along came the railways. When the OWW was being planned, here was a ready made branch to Stratford-on-Avon and in 1852/3 the railway company spent £1,486 on converting the tramway to standard gauge as was the main line. However, traffic was still drawn by horses belonging to private operators. The opening of the line from Honeybourne to Stratford-on-Avon in 1859 meant that one half of the tramway was redundant. The tramway provided a useful service for the places en-route with all southbound services in the morning, and the afternoon used for northbound ones. And so things would have remained, if the threat from another railway had not raised its head – the East & West Junction Railway was a bankrupt company, which was ripe for the LNWR or MR to take over, in this GWR heartland. Overcoming various oddities in the original Act of Parliament, such as not permitting steam engines, the GWR brought the line and buildings up to standard, reopening it on 1 July 1889. Four mixed trains ran in each direction. There were seven level crossings, all worked by the train crew and the line had steep gradients, for example 2½ miles of 1 in 68, bits at 1 in 58 and finally a drop to the terminus at 1 in 81. None of this was conducive to running the fast trains that passengers wanted. Also, most people went to Stratford as their main centre, not Moreton. By rail this would have necessitated three different trains. Wartime economy measures reduced the service by half and, although there was a small revival after the Great War, the passenger service ceased on 7 July 1929. A substitute bus service lasted less than four months. Trains were hauled by 0-6-0ST or 'Dean Goods' engines. Although the two intermediate stations were closed during the Second World War freight trains served Shipston-on-Stour right up until 2 May 1960.

Below: Where the line crossed the Fosse Way, a small passenger platform and a single siding were built, opening as Stretton-on-Fosse.
Lens of Sutton

Above: At Longdon Road, the original tramway curved north to Stratford. The GWR built a new curve to the south to allow direct Moreton to Shipston running. A single platform and two sidings, again adjacent to the level crossing, were provided. *Lens of Sutton*

Below: The terminus at Shipston-on-Stour, almost nine miles from Moreton, consisted of a single passenger platform, complete with engine release loop, engine shed, goods shed and several sidings. *Lens of Sutton*

Above: **Blockley, around 1920.** Where a secondary road crossed the line on the level was seen as a suitable opportunity for the OWW to build a station, albeit over two miles from the village of the name. This view is towards Worcester – probably little had changed between opening on 4 June 1853 and closure on 3 January 1966. The signal box dates from 1918, replacing an earlier one on the same site. Beyond the crossing gates can be seen the small goods shed, behind which were private sidings for Blockley Brick & Tile Co. When the line was being built, the then Lord Redesdale of Batsford Park (now Batsford Arboretum) near Blockley stipulated one concession the railway company would have to make if it wanted to pass across his land – every passenger train would stop at Moreton-in-Marsh. They still do. North of Moreton – at Aston Magna – a small private siding on the down side existed from 1902 for the Batsford Estates and Gloucestershire Brick Co. It closed, reopened, and was cut back before finally being removed in 1957. *Stations UK*

Below: **Chipping Campden, around 1960.** An excess of motive power in the form of 'Castle' Class 4-6-0 No.7019 *Fowey Castle* – with its shed plate missing – restarts a local stopping train towards Oxford. The connection from the down line, with its slip, installed in 1903, and ground signal to the up line, shows how goods sheds were accessed. *R S Carpenter collection*

Above: **Chipping Campden, 21 July 1963**. At opening on 4 June 1853 the OWW called this station Mickleton, but it changed to Chipping Campden, then Campden until February 1952, when it reverted to the name shown here. Although on the outskirts these days, when opened it was a good mile or so from the town. On the Oxford platform, on the right, is the original OWW building. By 1884 regulations demanded that crossings needed to be manned and so the signal box was built.   *R M Casserley*

Below: **Chipping Campden, 21 July 1963**. Looking towards Oxford provides a good picture of the goods shed and its connections. Note the loading gauge outside the shed and the fancy chimney stacks on the passenger building. Further along the line, beyond the shed, there was a connection, originally to Chipping Campden Gas & Coke Co. Ltd., later CC Coal, Coke & Lighting Co. Ltd., while on the up side another private siding was for agricultural use. The line is flat at this point. The station was closed on 3 January 1966.   *R M Casserley*

Cotswold Country

The GWR's literature on the Cotswolds – *'Cotswold Ways'*, 1924, *'The Cotswold Country'*, 1936, detailed articles, as in *'The Unknown Cotswolds'*, GWR Magazine, 1935 and the extensive coverage in the annual guide, *'Holiday Haunts'* – indicated the significance of this region for tourist traffic and for the company's celebration of Englishness. The Cotswold landscapes drew the attention of many writers well outside the sphere of railways, particularly through the inter-war era but the GWR's work is interesting, not least, for its particular thematic focus; its specific emphasis on a landscape and way of life that was largely beyond railways. *'The Unknown Cotswolds'* was prescriptive:

> Life in the Cotswolds is peaceful. Its quiet culture and harmonious beauty can only be taken in long, slow draughts, and not gulped at fifty miles an hour... travel by rail to the fringe of the Cotswolds and then go quietly through the peaceful lanes with no thought of anything so soul-destroying as a mileage schedule.

This essential theme had been pursued in the earlier work *'Cotswold Ways'* where there was also an emphasis upon the discriminating selective visitors conversant with the essential character of the area. Of Chipping Campden it was declared:

> If Campden should be invaded by the multitude, its charm and sanctity would flee. Fortunately, its beauties cannot be seen by motoring or rushing through it. It needs careful preparation and humble entry on foot. There is no entertainment other than for modest visitors.

Maxwell Fraser's work, *'The Cotswold Country'* showered praise upon Chipping Campden. Noting its location on the main Oxford-Worcester railway line she went on to register the historical and aesthetic qualities of this GWR showpiece:

> Outwardly Chipping Camden shows but little sign of the three hundred years and more since the majority of these lovely houses were first built, for it lies in the fold of the hills, away from the main roads. It has escaped the modern craze for change and has chosen the better part of peaceful contentment and enduring beauty.

The architectural heritage was underlined, and, as Fraser emphasised, was unspoiled. Harmony and continuity with the past was preserved:

> Nowhere can the Cotswold style of architecture, with its mullioned windows, grey slate roofs weathered to mellowness, dormered gables and graceful doorheads be seen to such perfection as at Chipping Campden where no jarring note of

modernity has been allowed to mar the gracious beauty of the wide main street or the picturesque grouping of the alms-houses and the great gateway of the magnificent church ... one of the loveliest of all the noble Cotswold church towers ... well worthy of the wealthy and important town it was designed to serve.

A 'beautiful Market Hall with its open archways', the Town Hall 'with its ancient buttresses', the Noel Arms 'which has a continuous existence as an inn since the 14th century', a Grammar School 'which retains some of its original buildings' and founded in 1487, together with 'the great 14th century house built by William Greville, one of the most famous wool-merchants of Chipping Campden' were further leading examples of the town's historic architecture. This litany of excellence was continued at nearby Broadway, served directly by the Birmingham-Stratford-Upon-Avon-Cheltenham line. The focus here, however, was somewhat different as Broadway was extensively identified as 'popular'.

The GWR identified the Cotswolds with the characteristics of Englishness in explicit statements as that carried in an article in the company magazine for

May, 1934. Entitled 'Half-Day Summer Holidays' it was aimed at those, 'who from lack of time, money and other considerations are prevented from enjoying the usual annual holiday'. It was unequivocal:

> No-one who calls himself a true Englishman can ever tire of the Cotswold country'.

But Broadway represented something of a 'frontier' culturally, whereby exclusive perspectives confronted more populist identifications. 'The Ward-Lock Guide to the Cotswolds', in the 1950s, described Broadway as 'A pleasant place which has the misfortune to be popular ...' whilst 'Holiday Haunts', 1936, identified Broadway as 'the most famous village in the Cotswolds'. Both 'Cotswold Ways', 1924, and 'The Cotswold Country', 1936, focused upon the church and its definitively rural-historical character. 'Cotswold Ways' rejoiced in the fact that it 'has not materially changed since Wycliffe's day and that it looked, as grey as now in Bloody Mary's time ...'. 'The Cotswold Country' concentrated upon historical detail:

> It was founded in 689 and contains a small brass dated 1572; a 14th century pulpit, an old Pillar alms box and a register dating from 1539 ...

Whilst Broadway was popular and easily accessible, Burford, mid-way between Oxford and Cheltenham was reached by the GWR's bus service from Oxford. A regular motor service, weekdays and Sundays, and through-ticket facilities, first and third classes, from Paddington and Reading were available. Likewise, combined road-rail excursions between London, Oxford and Cheltenham offered the opportunity of a circular trip through the Cotswolds. Shipton, to the north-east of Burford, was the closest main line station. 'The Unknown Cotswolds' celebrated the village for its magical atmosphere conveyed in terms of colour, textures and elevations which were best appreciated by following the clearly structured itinerary:

> ... it is one of those temperamental places that must be approached with infinite tact. Firstly you must come to it from the top end – it is a tragic waste to see it for the first time from the bottom of the hill – and you will be entranced by the sheer magic of the scene.

The impressionistic qualities were evident in further description from the article. Again, looking down the main street it continued:

> Uneven rows of houses, many of them typical of the gabled grace of the fifteenth century, flank the wide street with the noble church and river bridge standing proudly at the foot of the hill. It is a tone picture of grey and brown, here and there brightened by a flash of red or blue from a sign swinging outside a house or shop, the whole set off by the broad green verge running down the hill. The magic of Burford is most potent on a misty day for then the haze and the pennons of gently rising smoke soften the scene into one of harmonious loveliness. In any case Burford cannot be overlooked if only because of its church, which could provide an object lesson for almost every page of British history since the Saxons.

In summary, the GWR literature of the Cotswolds celebrated the region's definitive properties of Englishness. The historical and deeply rural nature of the landscape was presented within the company's cultural agenda of harmony and continuity, the thematic focus of all the material considered here. Parallels with GWR work on Somerset were evident, particularly that by Maxwell Fraser, who frequently drew on the imagery of 'haunts of ancient peace' and undisturbed harmony between man and nature and past and present to convey the essential spirit of the region or community. Landscape in the company's literature generally was never mere scenery or description; it was imbued with historical, political, cultural and aesthetic perspectives inherent in the collective expression of national identity. These gave the GWR literature its strong thematic focus which, combined with its evident narrative style, distinguished the company's work amongst the major companies during the inter-war era.

road leftward will bring the rambler to Moreton-in-Marsh, but for more footpath and less road follow the iron fence and subsequent hedge on the left of the park to a swing gate. The forward path from this will lead through more swing gates and over stiles to a back road of the town, where go ahead, turning left in the main street and right to the station.

RAMBLE No. 14

CAMPDEN STATION, MORETON-IN-MARSH, BOURTON-ON-THE-HILL, BLOCKLEY AND CHIPPING CAMPDEN
(8½ or 14 miles)

THIS ramble can be started either from Campden or Moreton-in-Marsh Station, according to whether the walker is coming from the Birmingham, Worcester or Oxford direction and the 8½-mile alternative is effected by starting at Moreton and finishing at Campden.

From the front or down side of Campden Station, (4) turn left past the gas works into the Paxford road, where turn left again, cross over the railway, take the right fork in a good half mile and continue to the bridge over Knee Brook. Ascend the tree-shaded hill beyond, turn right into Paxford, avoid another right turning, shortly bear left and follow this road for about 1½ miles. There is no need to apologise for this stretch of road, for it is winding and undulating, affords pretty views and soon becomes a mere lane, crossed here and there by gates. On nearing Aston Magna, where a Norman doorway will be found as part of two cottages, bear right with the road and at the church take the forward road, signposted "Moreton-

76

in-Marsh," but leave it shortly for a lane or track forking left.

At the railway bridge, pass under it and bear leftward near the railway, but veering from it by the brook, shortly passing through an opening on the left and going rightward over the hill. Pass through a small gate, continue forward, right of a low hedge and some trees, cross a stile and follow the path a little right of the railway. Cross the road at the hamlet of Dorn and take the forward lane or track, carrying on by the straight path from the right-hand of two gates for half a mile to a road. The

77

railway. After the latter has crossed the Stour, a swifter flowing river than the Avon, the path also crosses it by an iron footbridge and later passes under the railway. Turn left beyond it to a stile by the embankment, from which the path runs by the river for about a mile, later passing pleasantly between the trees and bushes nearer the water.

On reaching the open, the river bears away from the path, but is reached again at the railway bridge, which pass under and through the white swing gate on the right, following the riverside path and crossing the bridge later into the main road. Proceed along this successively through Bridge Street, Wood Street and Greenhill Street to the station, nearly a mile through the town. (2)

Extract from *Rambles in Shakespeare Land and the Cotswolds* published by the GWR in 1938.

Chipping Campden.   Chas. H.J.Mayo.

Above: **Campden Tunnel, c.1900.** A gang of navvies poses for the photographer outside one of the tunnel's portals. Quite what this occasion was or the date it took place seems to have been lost in the mists of time, but it was certainly less fraught than when pitched battles took place here in the years of the railway's construction – not a magistrate, soldier or wounded navvy in sight.

A Baker/Kidderminster Railway Museum

Campden Tunnel
Battle at Mickleton, 1851

The construction of the tunnel typified the way things were done on this line and many other early railway undertakings. Although started in 1846, progress was slow, contractors fell out and new partnerships took over while work stopped at times. It also illustrates the dictatorial attitude of directors, anxious for a return on their investment. What is different in this case is the scale of the problems faced to restart the work and that the great Brunel himself became involved in the dispute. On at least two occasions, the Riot Act was read by magistrates, and police and soldiers from the Gloucestershire Artillery were called. The contractor was defeated and the directors took over the contract, with the tunnel opening in the spring of 1852.

The original construction contract for the Campden tunnel and its approaches was held by Gale & Warden, passing in February 1847 to Williams, Aykroyd & Price. However, the tunnel became seriously behind schedule. Williams found a new partner, Marchant, but in June 1849 the OWW was forced to suspend construction due to financial problems, something common to many railway projects. In June 1851 the contractors were told to increase their workforce to get more work done or quit. The next month, the OWW's agent put in a sub-contractor to help with Marchant's section. However, the original workers felt they were being replaced and refused to work with the new navvies. Magistrates and sworn-in special constables helped keep the two sets of workers apart on 11 June, Brunel himself arriving later in the evening. The next day, both sides thought that an early start would give them a march on their competitors. The magistrates read the Riot Act leading to an uneasy peace between the two sides. One side occupied the site and the other side looked for opportunities to break in: this situation lasting for over a week. Brunel decided to flood the area with workers from the firm of Peto & Betts (numbers varied between 500 and 2,000 according to various reports) arriving on Sunday evening 20 July. The magistrates got wind of this gathering of workers and the possible implications and so in the very early hours of the next morning arrived with policemen and soldiers. So, in a deep cutting close to the Mickleton Road, a running battle ensued with the Riot Act being read again. Brunel's tactic worked and arbitration followed.

Above: **Campden tunnel, 1964**. This nicely shaped portal is the southern end of the 887' tunnel through a small outcrop of the Cotswolds. The photo was taken from the cab of a Hymek diesel: they were extensively used on the line in the late 1960s and early 1970s. There is now only one track through the tunnel, and since 1971, also for the fifteen miles from Evesham to Moreton. *Author's collection*

Above: **Emerging from Campden Tunnel.** 'Castle' Class 4-6-0 No.7023 *Penrice Castle* has just come out of the tunnel with an up express. Apart from a little switchback at 1 in 150 or so, it is downhill from Campden to Blockley, then up to just before Moreton-in-Marsh, and then down again for the 26 miles to Wolvercot Junction at an approximately average incline of 1 in 330, or 16' per mile. This is the reward for following river valleys: the North Midland Railway from Derby to Leeds avoided some large centres of population following the river valleys at a similar gradient. *P J Sharpe*

Campden Bank, 25 May 1963. An up freight headed by a 'Modified Hall' is about to enter the tunnel, assisted by No.2246.

M Mensing

Above: **Campden Bank, 1960s**. Judging from the smiling engineman, everything is well under control as No.7002 *Devizes Castle* ascends the bank on a London express. 7002 looks immaculate as one would expect at the time with a Worcester based express engine, though it only transferred there in December 1959. Prior to that it was a South Wales loco, based mainly at Landore, and that shed's 'Castles' positively gleamed, so Worcester had a good example to follow.

Author's collection

SPECIAL INSTRUCTIONS FOR ASCENDING INCLINES

From HONEYBOURNE, LITTLETON & BADSEY, EVESHAM or LONG MARSTON

To CHIPPING CAMPDEN or MORETON-IN-THE-MARSH

In order to save banking power as far as possible, Guards of trains must advise their Drivers particulars of the load at the last point at which the train is made up, and ascertain whether assistance will be required from Honeybourne, (1) to Chipping Campden only, (2) to Chipping Campden only, providing train is given a run through Blockley, or (3) to Moreton-in-Marsh, and Guards must give this information to the Inspector or Shunter in charge, who will be responsible for advising Honeybourne by telephone.

The Foreman or Signalman, according to circumstances, at the point where the assistant engine is attached, must advise the Chipping Campden Signalman the point to which the assistant engine is proceeding.

The assistant engine will not be coupled to these trains to Chipping Campden, except when it is working in the rear from Littleton and Badsey, Evesham or Long Marston, but in the event of the trains requiring assistance through to Moreton-in-Marsh in consequence of a clear run not having been obtained through from Chipping Campden to Moreton-in-Marsh the Signalman at Chipping Campden, after the train has come nearly to a stand at his Home Signal, must allow it to draw forward, stop it at the Signal Box, and so advise the train engine Driver, who must then give four crows on his engine whistle to indicate to the Guard and assistant engine Driver that the assistant engine is required to be attached, and when the latter has been coupled to the train, the assistant engine Driver must acknowledge the whistle by repetition.

In the event of a freight train being brought to a stand on the Loop Line at Honeybourne South Loop Junction Up Home Signal, and requiring the assistance of the assistant engine therefrom, the latter must be sent to Honeybourne East Loop Junction to enable it to get to the rear of the train.

Freight trains from the Birmingham District running via Honeybourne South Loop Junction and requiring an assistant engine will be advised to Honeybourne and Control by the starting point or last picking-up point.

Campden Bank, 31 May 1963. Ex-GWR 2-8-2T No.7218 is climbing towards Oxford. However, it is not deemed powerful enough on its own and so assistance is provided by a banking engine, '2251' class 0-6-0 No.2222. The train includes iron ore empties on their way back from South Wales to the Banbury area.

Kidderminster Railway Museum Trust

Banking engines based at Honeybourne, 1955/56

STATION	Engine No.	Starting Time	AUTHORISED HOURS							Total Hours per Week	PARTICULARS OF WORK
			Mon.	Tues.	Wed.	Thur.	Fri.	Sat.	Sun.		
Honeybourne ...	3	7. 0 a.m.	9	9	9	9	9	9	—	54 0	Shunting, Banking and Tip Working. Leaves Worcester Shed 5.55 a.m. daily. Runs to Littleton and Badsey at 4.0 p.m. for Shunting, thence to Evesham to take up working of Evesham No. 3 Engine.
	4	11. 0 p.m.	1	10½	10½	10½	10½	9½	—	52 30	Engine of 7.40 p.m. **SX** Worcester to Honeybourne banking and shunting as required. Works 9.30 a.m. Honeybourne to Worcester **MX**. Leaves Worcester Shed at 8.10 a.m. to work 9.30 a.m. Honeybourne to Worcester **MO**.

The descent into the River Severn valley is a different matter from the almost leisurely climb from Oxford. It is down at 1 in 100 for almost 4½ miles with about half a mile in tunnel. Gradients are a cause for concern for the operating side of a railway undertaking. There are three sets of catch points on the climb up so that if a train does split then the runaway wagons come off the line at the points rather than carry on down and into another train.

Below: **South of Honeybourne, 1958.** Having raced down the bank from the tunnel, an express for Worcester, hauled by a 'Castle', is about to pass under the road bridge and burst through the station at Honeybourne. The 1909 controlling signal box – 'Station South' – is mostly obscured by the exhaust from the engine. The double junctions seen allow transfer between what are, in reality, two parallel routes, the main line curving to the right in the background while the branch to Stratford-on-Avon curves to the left. Due to sighting difficulties caused by the road bridge on which the photographer is standing, the up starter signals pivot almost half-way along the arm rather than at the end which is the normal practice. To go to Cheltenham, trains would take the line to Stratford and then, just out of sight, at North Loop Junction, swing south to join the main line from Stratford at West Loop Junction, almost underneath the main line from Oxford. On the right is a siding and, between it and the train, the down goods loop. Trains having come down the bank would be able to stop here to unpin the brakes that had been applied at the top.

A W V Mace Collection, Mile Post 92½ Picture Library

Honeybourne, 1959. At opening, the single line was of mixed gauge with a passing loop at the station. Later in the same year, the OWW added a second line, of standard gauge only, but had to suspend its use because according to the authorising Act of Parliament – it had to be mixed gauge. Accordingly, the second track was converted to mixed gauge and was used from August 1854. However, no broad gauge public train ever used the lines. The right-hand platform was the one that passengers from Oxford would alight at, serving the down main line. Even though the station became a junction from 12 July 1859 when the single line north to Stratford-on-Avon opened, there was only the one up and down platform at that time. Access was from the adjacent road bridge by steps down to the platforms. The additional platforms were created in 1903/4. As the nameboard proudly proclaims, Honeybourne Junction was 'For Stratford-on-Avon Branch, Warwick, Leamington, Birmingham, Broadway, Winchcombe & Cheltenham' although the latter was not reached until 1906. Trains for the branches tended to use the north face of the island platform, No.3, or the new single platform, No.4 on the far left. An extensive new set of buildings was constructed to the south of the down line between the footbridge and the road bridge. Access to them all was by means of the large covered footbridge. The road bridge does cause signalling problems for up trains and so in the early 1930s the starter signal had a repeater arm hoisted high up to facilitate sighting, most un-GWR like. The publicity conscious GWR made great play of the fact that it served the 'Shakespeare Country' with excursions and coach tours. As at Kingham, the OWW was rather like a backbone with services radiating from it. The station closed on 5 May 1969, but reopened on 13 May 1985 with one, short, platform.

Stations UK

63

Above: **Honeybourne, late 1950s.** The canopies are doing a perfect job in protecting passengers from the rain. The various signs show up well. Waiting at platform 3 is the Cheltenham auto-train, with 0-4-2T No.1424. 85B Gloucester Horton Road was the 'home' for this engine, but it was sub-shedded at Cheltenham Malvern Road while working this service. These auto-trains gradually superseded the steam railcars that plied the branches from here to Stratford and Cheltenham. The facilities over on platform 4 were all in a multi-coloured brick building containing a waiting room, ladies room and at the other end, a gents toilet: there was no canopy. *David Lawrence*

Below: **Honeybourne, circa 1955.** Waiting at platform 3 again in anticipation of more travellers is a train for Stratford-on-Avon. '5101' class 2-6-2T No.4154 is in charge. Honeybourne had seen better times. Although more people used the station as a result of the new lines, stations and connections in the area, most freight and passengers were local. Approximately as many tickets were sold in 1903 as 1938, when one would have expected growth, and freight was only one-thirtieth of what it had been, resulting in the wage bill going from a contribution of around £14,000 to a drain of over £2,500. *A W V Mace Collection, Mile Post 92½ Picture Library*

Above: **Honeybourne, 1957**. The station is on one of the few pieces of flat ground on this line. It is sandwiched between, to the east, the almost four and a half miles at 1 in 100 gradient of Campden Bank, and to the west, a mile of 1 in 137 down, followed by a level stretch and then almost a mile down at 1 in 314. Given terrain like that, it is not surprising that eastbound freight trains have needed assistance right from the the OWW's opening day on 4 June 1853. Typical engines, even in the early days, were 0-6-0 tender engines; their servicing was done in a shed on the up side.

Enlargement of the station in 1907 resulted in the shed moving a little north, however it burned down four years later and so the GWR built this limited protection whilst coaling: the later brick office for the up sidings was a rest room for footplate crews. General improvements to the rail system including extra sidings, yards etc have already been alluded to. The provision of cycle storage here and at Crudington cost £251 in 1943.   *R S Carpenter collection*

STATION	Engine No.	Starting Time	AUTHORISED HOURS							Total Hours per Week		PARTICULARS OF WORK
			Mon.	Tues.	Wed.	Thur.	Fri.	Sat.	Sun.			
Honeybourne ...	1	5. 0 a.m.	19	24	24	24	24	24	6	145	0	Shunting Up Yard and banking as required. To Shed 6.0 a.m. Sundays.
	2	6. 0 a.m.	18	19¾	19¾	19¾	19¾	19¾	6	122	45	Shunting Down Yard and banking as required. To Shed 5.45 a.m. Tuesdays to Saturdays. Off pit 7.45 a.m. Tuesdays to Saturdays and works 9.15 a.m. Honeybourne to Long Marston and back. To Shed 6.0 a.m. Sunday.
	5	5.30 p.m.	7	7	7	7	7	1½	—	36	30	Shunting and banking. Engine of 3.5 p.m. Cheltenham to Honeybourne Freight. To Worcester Shed 12.30 a.m. Tuesday to Saturday and 7.10 p.m. on Saturdays. Engine may be ordered by Control to work trip to Worcester or Kidderminster, Tuesdays to Saturdays.
	6	6.30 a.m.	4½	4½	4½	4½	4½	4½	—	27	0	Evesham No. 2 Engine. Off Evesham Shed 5.45 a.m. Leaves Evesham for Honeybourne at 6.15 a.m. after berthing coaches of 7.3 a.m. Evesham Passenger in Up Shunting Spur. Works 8.15 a.m. Honeybourne to Littleton and Badsey returning to Honeybourne at 9||25 a.m. Leaves Honeybourne for Evesham at 12.30 p.m.

Shunting engines at Honeybourne, 1955/56

A few trains at Honeybourne, 28 June 1958.

Above: Large Prairie tank No.6106 accelerates away from the station on a stopping train to Oxford, where it is shedded.

E R Morten

Below: An unidentified 'Hall' 4-6-0 has charge of train 978, probably a Portsmouth to Birmingham working, composed mainly of Southern Region carriages.

E R Morten

Above: BR Standard 2-6-0 No.78009 – seen on Kingham shed earlier in the book – coasts into Honeybourne on the down main line with the daily pick-up freight. *E R Morten*

Below: One of Worcester shed's 'Castle' 4-6-0s passes the same signal gantry as 78009, but with a clear road, on a down Hereford express; it will not be stopping at the station here. *E R Morten*

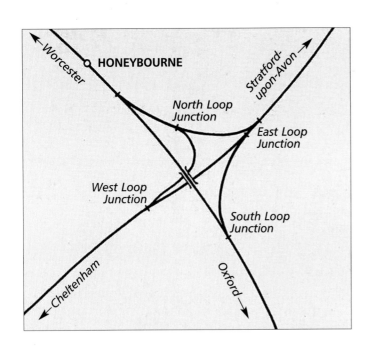

Branch to Stratford-on-Avon

Although the OWW obtained powers to build a line to Stratford-on-Avon in 1846, Honeybourne started as a country station from the opening of the line in 1853, on one of the few pieces of flat terrain. It became a junction in 1859 when a 9½ mile single line branch was built from the south of Honeybourne station curving north-east to Stratford-on-Avon with platforms at Long Marston and Milcote. The line was doubled in the 1900s as it became part of the through route from Birmingham to Cheltenham and Bristol. In 1941/2 a series of loops were built south of Long Marston station and were used as exchange sidings for an Army depot developed here. The depot had extensive sidings and loops, with its own locomotives and two platforms for passengers. The BR line was singled in 1980.

Below: Worcester based 0-6-0PT No.7777 heads a local passenger train which has come off the Stratford line and is approaching the station.
E R Morten

Above: **Stratford Racecourse station, circa 1955**. The GWR main line from Birmingham to Cheltenham rivalled the MR line and the notorious Lickey incline. On Summer Saturdays during the post Second World War period, both lines were worked to capacity by the sheer number of extra trains ferrying people to England's top holiday attractions in Devon and Cornwall. Having passed over a nine arch viaduct and crossed the River Avon on a steel bridge, this Paignton-Wolverhampton express from the south is passing through Racecourse station, with an unidentified 'Hall' class 4-6-0 in charge. *A W V Mace Collection, Mile Post 92¹/2 Picture Library*

Below: **Stratford-on-Avon, 1950s**. This St Austell-Birmingham express has just gone under the former Stratford & Midland Junction Railway line. Ahead is the station which was rebuilt in 1907 to give an up platform of 600 feet and a down one of 550 feet – long enough to cope with relief trains, often 12 coaches long. Hauling the train is 4-6-0 No.6995 *Benthall Hall*. *A W V Mace Collection, Mile Post 92¹/2 Picture Library*

Above: **Stratford-on-Avon, circa 1930s**. The OWW built a terminus at Sanctuary Lane, opening it on 12 July 1859. However, entering the town from the north, off the main Birmingham – London line, was a branch from Hatton, terminating at Birmingham Road from May 1860. The two lines became linked and so from 1 January 1863 a new through station opened with both termini closing to passengers. This view from the Alcester Road bridge is north.

Stations UK

Branch to Cheltenham

The GWR's need for a direct line to compete with the Midland Railway for traffic from Birmingham to Bristol was a point for much discussion in the company's boardroom. However, the cost and the work necessary for making the line, including the demolition of residential property in Cheltenham, meant putting off the idea. But eventually, the just over twenty-one miles line from Honeybourne to Cheltenham was built between 1904 and 1906. This was followed by the doubling of the Honeybourne to Stratford-on-Avon line and a connection across the main Worcester to Oxford line. Curves were also built at Honeybourne to allow many permutations of service. In 1908 the GWR started to use the route for through trains from Birmingham to Cheltenham, Bristol and the West Country. Iron ore traffic from the quarries around Banbury to the steel works in South Wales was one of the staple loads for the line. The rural nature of the area would have made it

more suitable to the development of a light railway, if the competitive desire to build a through route had not been there. When the connections between Cheltenham and Stratford were finished there were curves from that line to Honeybourne station as well as an east loop that allowed trains to come down the OWW and proceed north to Stratford without the need for stopping and reversing in the station.

For just under half a mile at the start of the line to Cheltenham, BR opened four up and four down loops in 1960, but they were short-lived, being taken out of use in 1966. However, four years later, the down loops were rebuilt but were not connected to the main line at their southern end. They survived a little longer, finally being closed in 1981. The line continued to be used by passenger trains until 1968 and freight trains until August 1976 when a derailment closed it. And so it remained until preservationists came along in the early 1980s to relay and reopen parts of the route, starting from Toddington.

Above: **Honeybourne, 14 August 1965**. The OWW bridge over the line to Cheltenham was a good vantage point to observe the best of both worlds. Here is the 12.30pm from Penzance to Wolverhampton hauled by Class Five 4-6-0 No.45006. It is passing over the points that make up Honeybourne West Loop Junction. As indicated by the points and the signals in the background, the train is to take the West loop towards Stratford. The other route from here curved up to join the OWW line at Honeybourne station. *M Mensing*

Below: **Weston-sub-Edge, 18 July 1959**. A southbound freight is passing the 400 feet platform being hauled by 2-8-0 No.3860. Just over two miles south of Honeybourne this station was originally known as Bretforton & Weston-sub-Edge, opening in 1904 when the line was constructed as far as Broadway, and later the same year to Toddington. The station lost the first part of its name in 1907. It closed to passengers in March 1960. *H C Casserley*

Above: **Littleton & Badsey, 1930**. The GWR opened a station at Blackminster siding and crossing on 21 April 1884 – but preferred to call it Littleton & Badsey. A 'Saint' 4-6-0 prepares to stop with a long Oxford bound train. Note how the tracks appear further apart than necessary, a throwback to the mixed gauge requirements. Interestingly, the station still had wooden buildings as, in 1872/3, the GWR rebuilt many stations in fancy brick. There was a fire here on 1 January 1890. In 1911 the platforms were extended at the eastern end. *Stations UK*

Left: **Littleton & Badsey, 1930s**. On the left is the original siding, now an up loop, with a shunting spur at the western end. The goods yard is well used, sidings being authorised in 1895 (1) and more in 1909 (2). The signal arm with a hoop on it is for controlling shunting movements; just in front of the train is the trailing slip connection between the up/down lines and the up loop. The station closed on 3 January 1966. *R S Carpenter collection*

As part of the wartime alterations a dispersed army storage depot was opened at Sheenhill about a mile west of Honeybourne station. Situated on the up side it consisted of four loops and several sidings with some engine support facilities. These serviced the depot which opened in 1944. The signal box closed in 1951 after which the sidings were progressively removed, remodelled and finally closed in 1965.

Above: **Aldington, 1960**. With Evesham a mile behind it, and on a very gentle falling gradient, No.7027 *Thornbury Castle* in charge of the up 'Cathedrals Express' will be expected to make good speed for although the train is only nine coaches long, Campden Bank, ahead, will tax it. From 1957 this was one of the expresses that travelled the line between Paddington, Oxford, Worcester and Hereford. The 8.0am from Hereford and 5.15pm from Paddington lost the name in 1965 but were known by it for many years. In 2001 the name appears in the timetable again with the up train taking 2 hours 44 minutes and the down train 2 hours 50 minutes. These are about 40 minutes faster than the 1949 times. *Author's collection*

Below: **Aldington sidings, 1926**. About half way between Littleton and Evesham a loop was built by 1883 to serve a loading bay. Fifteen years later authorisation was obtained to extensively enlarge the layout. Summer fruit was the main trade – the Vale of Evesham, being in the River Severn flood plain, possesses fertile soil and is sheltered by the Cotswolds and Bredon Hills. Although gooseberries mature in June, and strawberries a little later, together with currants of various colours, it was the plum traffic in August and early September when the sidings here were chiefly used. Pershore, Evesham, and, later, Toddington, were all rail centres for the traffic with the sidings here providing extra capacity to relieve congestion and, from the GWR's point of view, beating the competition of the Midland Railway in the area. Full van consignments went to Liverpool, Manchester and, via the GCR at Banbury, Leicester and Sheffield. Worcester was the local railhead for less than van loads. Road competition was responsible for its closure in 1959. *R S Carpenter collection*

Below: **Evesham, 4 June 1963**. The town of Evesham is focused around a bend in the River Avon, indeed it is the presence of the river in the lea of the Cotswolds that makes the area fertile and famous for its market gardening. In 1934 the station handled over 60,000 tons of freight which may not appear much when compared to Kidderminster's half a million tons, but when viewed against other stations along the line, such as Adlestrop – 1,433 tons – then it was quite an amount. Therefore it was only natural that when the OWW built a line through the area they built a station here, opening it on 1 May 1852. Most important trains stopped here, including this London to Worcester service with No.7023 *Penrice Castle* in charge. Goods facilities at Evesham were on the down side: a loading dock and cattle pens to the east of the station with the goods shed to the west. Both were sandwiched in by the adjacent Midland station to the south-west. By this time the goods shed's store had seen better times. Unlike other sheds along the line, the one here was not on a loop with access from both ends. The line to the left served a coal wharf at the up end, behind the 1901 platform. While the up platform was extended in 1901 to the east by the removal of the engine shed that was there, the down platform had this very narrow portion added adjacent to the goods shed. Surprisingly, a water column was squeezed in there too. It, and the one at the end of the up platform, was fed by the water tank on the left.   *R K Blencowe collection*

Left: **Evesham, August 1962**. Today this is the start of the single line to Moreton-in-Marsh – a case of history repeating the situation at opening in 1852. The express train for Worcester has just passed under the MR line which is carried by the bridge in the distance. The home signal controlling events has a white board behind the arm to make it show up better. On the right is the down refuge siding and another siding on the extreme right. To the left of the engine the up loop joins the main line. As the line is on a curve, the presence of the bridge from which this picture was taken makes seeing the controlling signals difficult, hence the distinctive one in the left foreground. The line now carries a 75 mph speed restriction.

A W V Mace Collection,
Mile Post 92¹/2 Picture Library

Right: Evesham station was spotlighted in the British Railways Staff magazine during the 1950s. Besides agricultural traffic, the locally made sausages were transported by rail. It was also a popular destination for days out from Birmingham.

Spotlight on Evesham

EVESHAM is a market town in the centre of the Vale of Evesham fruit and vegetable district. The river Avon is a great attraction to visitors, and on spring and summer bank holidays half a dozen trains may bring 2000 passengers from Birmingham and the Midlands. Evesham is one of the few places in England where two churches share the same churchyard, where formerly the abbey also used to stand in the precincts. Inwards freight traffic consists principally of fertilisers and coal. Fruit and vegetables are despatched to all parts of Great Britain by fast goods services. Outwards parcels traffic is chiefly sausages and soft fruit in season. Annual traffic totals are : Freight outwards, 22,000 tons ; inwards, 62,000. Parcels outwards, 143,000 ; inwards, 49,000. Passengers booked, 94,000 ; season tickets, 1000.

Portraits are of Station Master F. Ashworth, Booking Clerk R. Webb, Leading Porter J. Owens, and Ganger F. Haines (permanent Way).

Below: **Evesham, 14 April 1959**. The original wooden buildings were replaced by brick ones by the GWR which also built the covered footbridge. Note the white paint on the post on the right – painted like this during the Second World War to stop people walking into it during the black-out. 2-6-2T No.4152 from shed 85A, Worcester, is on the 12.9pm from Stratford-on-Avon, which took half an hour to here with this stopping train at platform 3: nos. 1 & 2 were the ex-Midland platforms. This was part of a harmonisation scheme when the Western Region took over the Midland station in 1958. On the far right is the majestic Railway Hotel. *B W L Brooksbank, Initial Photographics*

Above: **Evesham, 14 April 1962**. Passengers who boarded the 6.15pm at Worcester have just alighted. Prior to rebuilding, the passenger facilities were housed in a building similar to that still extant at Charlbury. Adjacent to that was a dip in the platform, and a barrow crossing. Passengers trying to get on and off coaches opposite this must have needed special assistance. The construction of the footbridge led to the raising of the platform and today's building. The diesel railcars are W38W & W33W. In 1942, W38 was built as one half of a double rail car set with W37. However, W37 caught fire on 18 February 1949 and so was removed. W33, a similar style car from 1941, was converted to replace it. This involved removal of one of the driving compartments so that it could be connected to W38; they offered 92 seats. The pair lasted until August 1962, by which time BR was modernising its diesel unit fleet with the experience gained from such experiments. *M Mensing*

Below: **Evesham, 1951**. The Midland Railway built an alternative route to the Lickey incline which went via Redditch to Ashchurch opening it in sections from 1859 and throughout in 1868. Although the line through Evesham is roughly, north-south, the station is east-west; in this way savings were made by having a common approach road etc., the two stations – GWR and MR – being across the road from each other. To the right can be seen the Great Western's on the line from Worcester to Oxford, complete with water tank. In the middle of the picture is the Midland Railway's station with lattice footbridge. The time is about a quarter to three. Fowler parallel boilered 2-6-4T No.42326 on the 2.20pm Ashchurch to Birmingham is filling up with water, while at the other platform is the 12.50pm Birmingham to Ashchurch. In 1866 a connection between the two companies was laid in the area south of the GWR goods shed. The line from Redditch to Evesham was single with loops at stations and junctions at Alcester. Due to the congestion that the Lickey incline caused, it was used as an alternative, being a less steeply graded line: the operational difficulty was that there was only single track. *Author's collection*

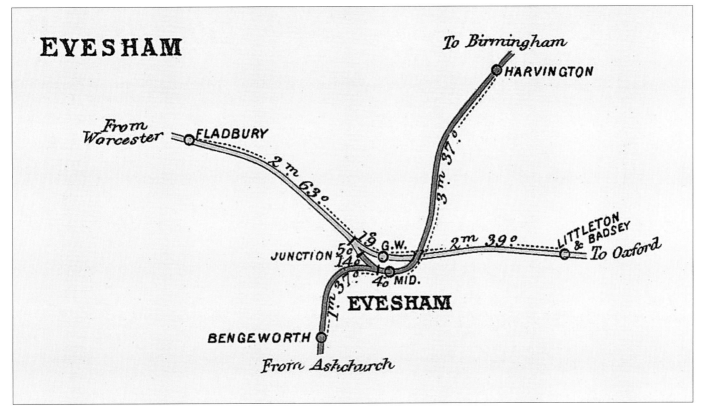

EVESHAM

To Birmingham

HARVINGTON

From Worcester

FLADBURY

2 m 63 c

3 m 37 c

18 G.W.

LITTLETON & BADSEY

2 m 39 c

To Oxford

JUNCTION 5 c

14 c

1 m 37 c

4 c MID.

EVESHAM

BENGEWORTH

From Ashchurch

Above: The junction at Evesham between the Midland Railway and GWR as it was in 1914.

Below: **Evesham, late 1950s.** Looking through the engine's smoke shows the OWW line curving away right towards Worcester. The 1866 connection between the MR and GWR, as shown in the above map, was found to be too complicated, so it was removed and, in 1957, a new junction was built. This involved the MR up line joining the GWR down line almost opposite the new signal box with its vertical wooden cladding. Then there was a trailing crossover so that trains could pass onto the GWR up line. For the opposite direction there was a trailing crossover on the MR lines just before the lines crossed the River Avon. Snaking its way at the 10 mph regulation speed off the Midland line from Ashchurch is a freight train hauled by GWR 2-8-0 No.2818. It is on the bi-directional loop and is about to cross onto the down main. The 1901 GWR engine shed, complete with engine *in situ* and parachute water tank, can be seen above the first few wagons: it closed in 1961. *Author's collection*

Above: **Evesham, October 1962**. Heading towards Oxford is a block train of oil tanks being hauled by 2-8-0 No.3840. The up goods loop, immediately behind the tanks, has a DMU waiting its next turn. In the rear is the now closed engine shed. To the right of the wagons is the 1957 signal box which controlled the signals in the foreground. In the background is the New Yard dating from 1926, extended and enlarged in 1930 and 1936. Shunting is in operation for the vans that carry produce from the Vale of Evesham's large market garden industry. A shed with loading platform is almost obscured by the bracket signal. *RAS Marketing*

Below: **Evesham, 1959**. Crossing the River Avon is Prairie tank No.4168. Originally there was a wooden viaduct here that was rebuilt after 1873. For over fifty years the only connections between the up and down lines was a trailing one in the station opposite the goods shed. The one here and the points for the up and down loops were all built in 1907 and the joining of the two lines is by a facing connection a short distance east of here: from 1971 the line has been single for the eight miles east to Norton Junction. East of the bridge was a loop on the down side which became a private siding for local firm Deakin and, later, G Swift in 1907. A signal box, Evesham North, opened then to control access and to be a block post. It closed in 1957 when the new Evesham box took over its functions and those of the South box, sighted at the eastern end of the down platform. The sidings were taken out of use in 1965. *Author's collection*

Above: **Fladbury, 15 June 1963**. It was on the near line that trains from Oxford stopped, the OWW opening the station on 1 May 1852. Steps led down to the platforms from the adjacent overbridge. A crossover was needed from 1879 when a siding, long loop and very long siding to Spring Farm Mill was developed. The platforms were authorised to be extended in 1883, the crossover was moved west and the siding made into a loop with the main line; a signal box was just to the left on the up side. Just under the bridge was a small loop and two sidings known as Charlton Siding, originating by 1882, then enlarged and added to in 1902 when a signal box was built to control events. The sidings were terminated in 1963, the box closed the next year and the station on 3 January 1966.   *R M Casserley*

Below: **Wyre Halt, 1961**. With the development of auto trains and diesel railcars, the GWR speculated that it could get more passengers by opening small unstaffed halts along its lines and this one opened on 11 June 1934. Access to the near platform, for Oxford, and the other one, was down a slope from the bridge. A lamp was provided on each platform, not always a feature of such halts. It would be the guard from trains stopping here who attended to the lamps. It closed on 3 January 1966. The nearest line is the one in use today.   *R M Casserley*

Above: **Pershore,18 July 1959.** The OWW station of 1 May 1852 is still open to passengers. Looking along the down platform, expecting a train from Oxford, shows the wooden goods shed on the loop. This was longer than the shed as there was a wharf for loading vegetable and soft fruit traffic, which was extended in 1887 and 1906. The eastern end of this platform was lengthened by 1901, the line from the goods shed being slewed outwards to accommodate this: a loading dock and cattle pens were also on this siding. The 1936 replacement for an earlier signal box has the up main signal cantilevered to aid sighting, and a smaller arm for the up loop which went around the platform. Some time between 1910 and 1912 the up platform was extended easterly as the change in levels shows. The passenger accommodation is in the form of a brick shelter with fine arched windows and door.   *R M Casserley*

Below: **Pershore, 1961.** The two sidings that have wagons in them were added in the mid 1920s when the up siding was converted into a loop around the platform, it was extended easterly in 1936. On the right was a large covering for the loading dock. Probably at the same time as the down platform was extended the opportunity to rebuild the station buildings in brick was taken by the GWR, which built the footbridge too. To celebrate the centenary of cultivation of the variety of plum grown locally, 'Bulldog' class 4-4-0 No.3353 was renamed *Pershore Plum*.   *R M Casserley*

Above: **Pershore, c.1935**. The GWR was not slow in adopting road transport to augment rail services and help it compete with road hauliers. In 1931, for example, it owned 1,324 goods and parcels motor vehicles for distributing goods from GWR railheads to places not served by train. There was a 52 page customer booklet entitled 'Door to Door by Country Cartage services' which listed the villages served and the scales of charges. This photograph shows the lorry driver, Harry Carter, receiving some paperwork for his cargo from his boss, Mr Powell, probably before setting out on his rounds of the small villages in the area. *A Baker/Kidderminster Railway Museum*

Below: **Pershore, c.1935**. The railway station is a goodly walk from the town, so the GWR's provision of a connecting bus service was a boon for passengers. Once again, Harry Carter is the driver, on the vehicle's steps, with Cartage Foreman Bert Griffin on the left and Stationmaster Mann on the right. The GWR was a pioneer, in 1903, among railway companies in utilising road motors as feeders to its system. Its road vehicle interests in the 1930s included a number of subsidiary bus companies including City of Oxford Motor Services Ltd.

A Baker/Kidderminster Railway Museum

Cathedral Line

Looking beyond the Cotswolds, Evesham and Worcester were the two notable locations at the western end of the Oxford-Worcester route. Here, the line also served the celebrated horticultural district of the Vale of Evesham, famous for its fruit production in particular and identified by the GWR General Manager, James Inglis, in 1904 as 'The Garden of England.'

Evesham was acknowledge for its historical record, 'Holiday Haunts', 1929, identified it as 'one of the most historical towns in the Midlands', extending back over twelve hundred years. The 1929 guide emphasised the legendary, romantic character of the town, in a detailed entry focusing on the magical origins of the famous abbey. By 1935, 'Holiday Haunts' had shifted its focus to a progressive historical outline, although the abbey remained a central feature.

For eight hundred years the history of Evesham was the history of its great abbey – a brilliant pageant in which saints and sinners, bishops, abbots, kings and nobles figure with a background of peace and prosperity, learning, fasting, miracles and warfare, and the ever-growing train of pilgrims until the final Dissolution.

The eighteenth century 'set a seal on its fair fame and made it as great a place for pilgrimage for tourists as it once was for those who crowded to the shrines of the abbey.' This pursuit of picturesque landscape with all its attendant historical associations marked the beginning of tourist activity, albeit on a highly exclusive basis, but it did establish the essential agenda, itinerary and protocol adopted by the GWR, particularly in its early period of tourist development. The sometimes almost impenetrable style and content of the company's earliest literature, in the pre-grouping era, was based very closely on late eighteenth and nineteenth century guide books. The largely exclusive character of much of the Cotswold work for example, reflects this.

'Holiday Haunts', 1935, indicated that the greater part of Evesham Abbey had been destroyed in the Dissolution under Henry VIII but the Bell Tower remained, 'conspicuously marking the site of the abbey ruins.' In summary, it was clear that the GWR wished to stress continuity of past and present: 'There are numerous ancient houses in Evesham, and the whole town has a fascinating air of dignity and age, blending with its cheerful modern hotels and shops.' Traditional England had to be complemented with the appropriate modern amenities as a principle in GWR marketing.

Pershore, between Evesham and Worcester, was situate in a landscape of 'orchards and gardens, fertile meadows and highly cultivated fruit plantations, on which, principally, grows the celebrated Pershore Plum, unrivalled amongst its species as a preserve. Here was started the first co-operative fruit market in the country which has now developed into the chief business of the neighbourhood.' This was the entry for the 1929 'Holiday Haunts', and in commercial terms, Pershore and the Vale of Evesham generally was of immense value to the GWR for its fruit traffic. But that same volume identified another feature of that district in terms of national significance, culturally. The entry is included here for its stylistic form and unequivocal sense of pride in association and inheritance:

But there is one thing in Pershore that speaks to the mind of magnificence departed, and this is the Church of Holy Cross which once formed part of the stately Abbey said to have been 250 feet long and

Evesham Bell Tower, from *Cotswold Ways*, 1924

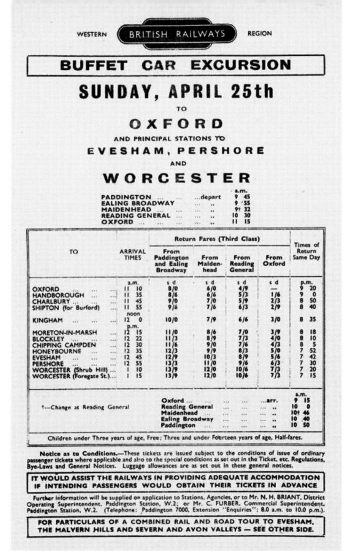

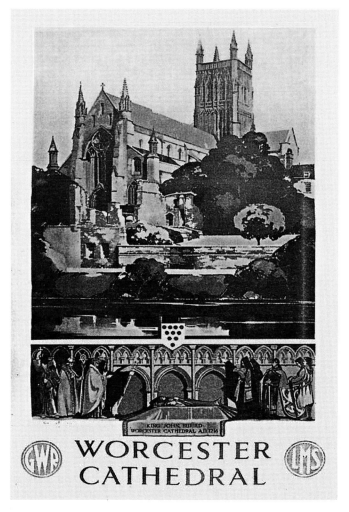

120 feet broad. In the lower part of the Severn Valley, and in that part of the Valley of the Avon as it nears the Severn lay, in pre-reformation days, the largest group of great abbeys throughout England. Today the neighbourhood is the richest in the country as to existing abbey churches. One of these is Pershore Abbey. The Norman nave went to ruin after the dissolution of the monasteries in 1539; its great north transept fell down in the seventeenth century. But what remains still forms a church of exceptional beauty, interest and value as an inheritance of the Anglican Church and as a national treasure.

Worcester provided the GWR with an abundance of historical interest. On a regional scale the city was considered to be 'one of the oldest, proudest and most interesting towns in the Midlands and the ideal capital for the medieval treasure house of Worcestershire.' 'The Severn Valley', 1923, one of the 'Handy Aids' series put it into a national and international context; conferring upon it 'that position as one of England's great travel shrines which the enthusiasm of overseas pilgrims has assigned to Chester, Oxford and Stratford-On-Avon.' 'The Severn Valley' devoted an entire chapter to 'Ever Faithful Worcester' and in conclusion declared the city to be 'one of the Empire's foremost travel shrines.'

The cathedral was the focal point and together with its history and particular setting was considered to represent a powerful expression of Englishness, a perspective emphasised in the literature:

The cathedral is distinguished from many of its rivals by what may be called 'the grace and dignity of its pose.' It stands so close to the riverbanks that its stately tower is often reflected in the placid waters of the Severn. The quiet beauty of College Green lends an additional charm to its situation, and the ivy-clad ruins of the Guesten Hall, the Infirmary and other portions of the original monastic buildings slope down to the water's edge.

Both 'Holiday Haunts' and 'The Severn Valley' enumerated the many historic buildings within the city, noting also that 'there are no less than eleven parish churches within the town...' whilst, 'in many streets it is more difficult to find the modern houses than those of centuries ago.' Moreover, Worcester was home to Royal Worcester china from the Royal Porcelain Works, founded in 1751, and host to the annual Hop and Ram fair, 'the only one of its kind in England, which has been held every year since the reign of Queen Mary', in the mid sixteenth century. Continuity and tradition prevailed.

Above: **Stoulton, around 1920.** A passenger looking this way would see trains from Worcester pull in to the other platform: before 20 February 1899 there was no station here. The one proposed was to be called 'Windmill End'. The brick buildings illustrate the GWR's attitude to smaller stations: provide decent facilities and when – not 'if' – passenger growth occurs you have a station to be proud of; note the provision of plenty of lamps and the distance between lines showing the planning for broad gauge. The milk churns on the up platform should be in the right place to be loaded into the appropriate van.   *Stations UK*

Below: **Stoulton, 1961.** A signal box at the eastern end of the up platform controlled events including this lower quadrant signal. For a few years there was a loop and siding east of the station on the down side. Closure was on 3 January 1966 and given the obvious rural nature of the area, the probably constant population numbers and the increasing threat from cars, it is not hard to see why.   *Stations UK*

Above: **Norton Junction, 17 April 1965.** Taking the line to Oxford is 'Modified Hall' 4-6-0 No.6967 *Willesley Hall* – though its nameplate is missing. The train is the 4.30pm from Worcester Foregate Street to Stratford-on-Avon, which took 66 minutes: today we would not tolerate such a long time for such a short journey. Norton Halt is just under the road bridge in the background – this train should have stopped there, but, according to the photographer, it did not! The line in the foreground is the short chord from the Midland Railway at Abbott's Wood Junction on the main MR line from Gloucester to Birmingham. *M Mensing*

Below: **Norton Junction.** From opening on 5 October 1850 until 7 September 1959 the station was called Norton Junction, then it changed to 'Norton Halt' until closure. This view is east, towards Evesham. The opening of this station, and Worcester's, for Birmingham-Gloucester trains, was far earlier than others on the OWW reflecting the complex railway politics of the times. The signals for the junction are up high for sighting purposes and it is the GWR route that is deemed to be the most important as its arm is highest. In later years, they would be placed at the same height. The controlling box, which is still there today, is hiding behind the bridge, beyond which is the spur to the Midland line to the right. For the travelling public, this was not a junction station. Although an MR local service was established between Gloucester and Worcester, its trains did not stop here latterly, being used only for GWR trains. *Lens of Sutton*

Above: **Norton Halt, 1961**. The photographer would have walked down a slope to get onto this, the platform for Worcester. As more passengers were expected on this side, it is where the main GWR brick building was situated, with Oxford bound travellers having to make do with a wooden shelter – even this had shrunk over the years before closure on 3 January 1966. Just visible on the right is the up refuge siding north of the station so that trains proceeding south onto the MR line could be set back and wait while a down train crossed the junction. It also provided a place to park freight trains while faster services overtook them.

Stations UK

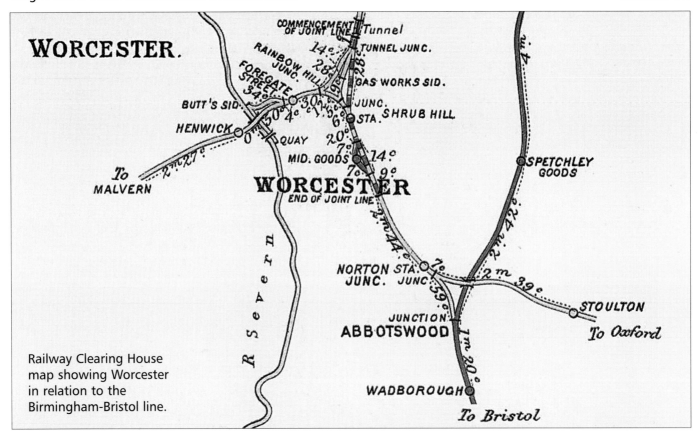

Railway Clearing House map showing Worcester in relation to the Birmingham-Bristol line.

Worcester

In pre-railway days Worcester was a great coach connecting place and a centre of commerce with its own cathedral. In the early 1840s the population was around 27,000, quite large for that era. However, it was rapidly overtaken by the new industrial towns. Anyone who knew of the meeting on 25 September 1835 of the committees, one from each place, to look into a Birmingham & Bristol Railway, held at a hotel in Worcester, may have thought the city was pivotal to the scheme. Nothing could be further from the truth. The plans agreed upon, except for a revision to include a detour via Cheltenham, were for today's line and avoided Worcester altogether. There followed many schemes, either to divert the main Birmingham Gloucester (B&G) line, or to have branches from it to serve Worcester, but none of them materialised. After opening of the B&G in 1840, a horse-drawn coach connected Worcester with the line at Spetchley, three and a half miles to the east. Four years and more schemes later, a Board of Trade inquiry resulted in the B&G being obliged to build a branch to serve the city, gas works and docks. But before an Act could be promoted, an earlier proposal to connect Worcester, Kidderminster and Stourbridge with the Grand Junction Railway at Wolverhampton under the title 'Oxford Worcester & Wolverhampton Railway' was revived. The venture was supported by the GWR as a mechanism for extending the broad gauge sphere of influence into the area. But the GWR's broad gauge ambitions for Worcester never came about. On 5 October 1850, the first section of the OWW, a single standard gauge line from Abbot's Wood on the B&G to Worcester Joint station, was opened and leased to the B&G and, later, the Midland Railway. The 'Worcester Journal' of 10 May 1850 told its readers:

...that this small instalment for placing Worcester on the same footing as other principal towns of the Kingdom... was accomplished...

serving to illustrate the esteem Worcester held in its inhabitants' eyes and why it had been such a problem to the B&G and, later, the Midland Railway. Trains for Birmingham ran from Worcester to Abbot's Wood, where they reversed and headed north through Spetchley until the OWW's northward deviation through Droitwich to meet the B&G at Stoke Works was completed in February 1852. The Midland then sent all its passenger trains through Worcester until 1880 when most workings reverted to the 'old road' via Spetchley. Despite all the problems, Worcester was quite a railway centre in steam days. It was chosen by the OWW as the site of its locomotive works. There was also a private loco building enterprise, The Worcester Engine Company, for a number of years, along with works for carriage and wagon construction and repairs, also for signalling, some owned by the GWR and others by private industry, all creating a lot of employment in the city. Worcester Engine Company, started by former managers of the West Midland Railway, had 750 employees in 1865 – it built 70 locos in the period to 1871 – but unfortunately went bust. The works passed to the West Central Wagon Co and then, in 1903, to Heenan & Froude. McKenzie & Holland, who made signalling equipment, employed 600 people in 1900. These enterprises were all close to Shrub Hill station, so along with the former OWW works, there was a substantial railway community in the area. Currently Worcester enjoys a healthy service on the OWW and from Birmingham to Hereford, but is still on the side lines for Birmingham-Bristol trains.

The allocation at WOS Worcester in June 1947	
4-6-0	23
4-4-0	2
2-8-0	7
2-6-0	9
0-6-0	15
2-6-2T	11
0-6-0T	19
0-4-2T	5
Diesel Railcar	7
Total	**98**

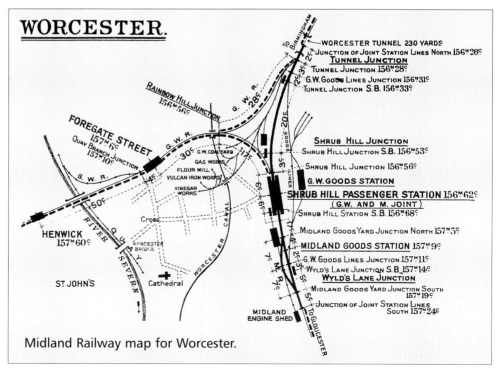

Midland Railway map for Worcester.

Above: **Wyld's Lane, circa 1960.** 'Modified Hall' No.7928 *Wolf Hall* is leaving Worcester with a southbound express. Wyld's Lane Junction was the meeting place of several lines in the area; the junction box is behind the rear coach. On the right are two containers – part of an initiative that failed to stem the loss of traffic to road transport. They are in the sidings of the Metal Box Company which date from 1930, put in at a cost of £1,655, with another £1,381 paid out to extend them later.

David Lawrence

Below: **Midland locomotive shed, 1937.** Although Worcester is often thought to be 'GWR territory', the Midland Railway had a substantial presence. Opposite Wyld's Lane signal box, and controlled by it, were the access to the MR's substantial goods shed (still standing) and an engine shed to the south. This wooden building opened in 1870, lasting until 1932. The shed closed due to traffic pooling arrangements between the 'Big Four' railways, which meant that LMS freight trains were no longer routed to South Wales via Worcester and Hereford. Upon closure the engines transferred to Gloucester LMS, except one duty, which needed the presence of a 4-4-0 in Worcester and so it used the GWR shed, where LMS locos became a familiar sight over the years. This site is now the Perrywood Trading Estate.

W A Camwell

Above: **Wyld's Lane, 1960**. The 1931 signal box here was very busy. It not only controlled the MR's connections to the joint main lines but also departures from the GWR's goods line that avoided Shrub Hill station on the way north to Tunnel Junction. Waiting by the water column is 4-6-0 No.4945 *Milligan Hall*. It is in charge of a Stourbridge Junction to Stoke Gifford freight. When the main line is clear, it will proceed east to Norton Junction and go down the MR main line to the Bristol area. The express, hauled by 'Castle' class 4-6-0 No.7007 *Great Western*, is the 11.50am Hereford to Paddington, away from Shrub Hill at 12.55pm and due in the capital at 3.25pm, taking about a hour longer than trains today.   *Unknown*

Below: **Worcester, 1 August 1960**. Two companies' goods sheds are in this view: the MR's is just visible on the left, opened in 1868, and the GWR's on the right. Sandwiched between the two are the main passenger running lines. The 12.33pm stopper to Evesham and Leamington hauled by 5700 Class 0-6-0 No.4614, ran ahead of the express seen in the previous picture, before turning off at Honeybourne to go to Stratford and Leamington.   *Author's collection*

Above: **Worcester Shrub Hill exterior, circa 1960**. The temporary station originally here was rebuilt in 1865 by the GWR, and is the one that substantially remains today. The line is on an embankment with the station being on the section between Newtown Road to the south and Tolladine Road to the north. An approach road from Shrub Hill Road, to the west, divides into two, each branch curving up and meeting outside the covered entrance to the station. It must have been quite imposing in the horse and carriage days; now it is a one-way street with vehicle parking ruining the impression. For passengers on foot, Shrub Hill station is some way from the town centre.   *R K Blencowe collection*

Below: **Worcester Shrub Hill, 5 August 1932**. Although mainly bypassed by north-south trains, the two companies made Shrub Hill into an impressive station. Basically, there were up and down main platforms with bays at each end. This arrangement allowed for the termination of services from all directions. Two central loops were also built, with crossovers to the platform lines, allowing separation and additions to trains. Between the two footbridges across the four tracks a train shed was developed for passenger protection – the central part was open to allow smoke and steam to escape. It was removed sometime after 1935. The main up platform is in view from which trains to Oxford would depart. Note the banner signals controlling the crossover. On the left are coaches in the shed / platform for Hereford local trains.
                                                        V R Webster, Kidderminster Railway Museum

Above: **Worcester Shrub Hill, 23 July 1961**. What a difference just over a generation makes! Worcester was, and still is, the home to an impressive display of semaphore signals; Shrub Hill Junction signal box is in the left background with the engine shed in the centre. The crossovers are well displayed and the removal of the roof has made the station light and airy. The signals for the central line, due to sighting problems, are now hoisted above any stock occupying the platform line. Prairie tank 2-6-2T No.6111 acts as the station pilot between other duties. A three-car DMU waits in the bay at the north end of platform 3. *R K Blencowe collection*

Below: **Worcester Shrub Hill, circa 1955**. This view is north from the end of the up platform. The signals with their back to us control entry to the platform or the central loop. Those facing us are for down trains, to Droitwich on the right, or Hereford on the left. All the main posts have a small 'calling on' arm on them: this allowed one engine to enter the section already occupied by another for shunting purposes. On the right are signals with a white hoop: this signified that they were for goods lines, being off to the right. The engine, 0-6-0PT No.1661, fitted with a spark arrestor, and coupled to a GWR shunting truck, is on the line connecting the Hereford sidings with the line which crosses the main line north, to Foregate Street station. The water tank fed the adjacent column, and others, removing the necessity for shunting and goods engines to go to the shed. *Author's collection*

Above: **Worcester Shrub Hill**. 'Hall' 4-6-0 No.4900 *St Martin*, the very first of this class of dependable GWR mixed traffic workhorses, trundles through the station with two coaches in tow, one a restaurant car, no doubt ready for attaching to the Hereford-London train. No.4900 was a Worcester based engine from July 1952 to June 1956.

Stations UK

Right: **GWR engines at Worcester**. Over the years, probably most classes of permitted GWR engines have made an appearance. As express trains became heavier, stronger engines were needed to haul them and to reduce journey times. The photograph of the 'Single' engine, 4-2-2 No.3031 *Achilles* dates from just before The Great War, while 4-4-0 No.4110 *Charles Mortimer* is from 1923. The 'Saint' class 4-6-0 is No.2944 *Highnam Court,* seen in the 1930s.

R S Carpenter collection /R K Blencowe collection /RAS Marketing

Below: **Worcester Shrub Hill, 11 June 1963**. Displaying express passenger train headcode is 'Castle' class No.7005 *Sir Edward Elgar* making its way off shed through the station for 1A85, the 3.10pm to London Paddington, which it will take over from the loco which brought the train in from Hereford. No.7005, a long-time resident of Worcester shed, was of course named in honour of the famous composer – though it started life called *Lamphey Castle*, being renamed in the 1950s. Hereford-Worcester-London expresses remained steam hauled later than many other parts of the Western Region and even after 'official' dieselisation of the service, steam often had to be recalled due to problems with the new motive power.

R K Blencowe collection

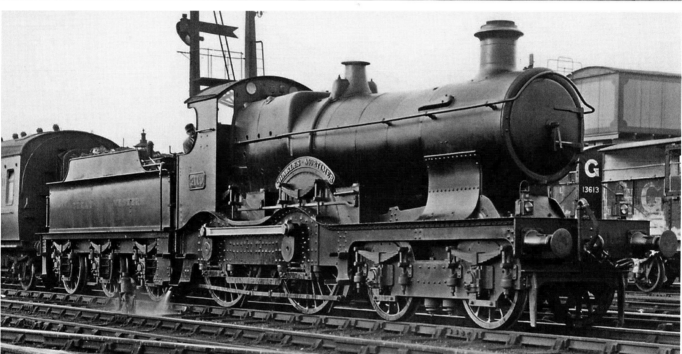

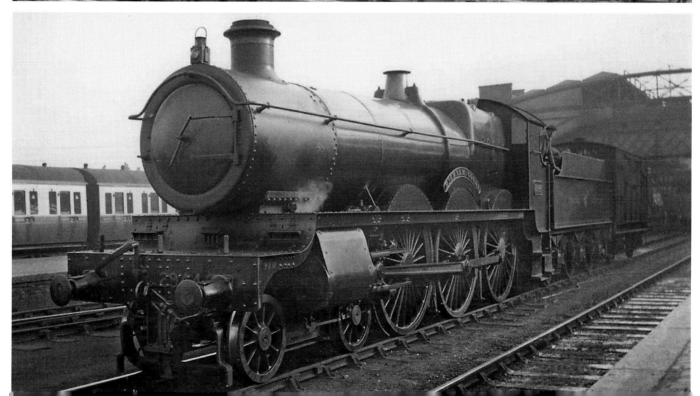

Above: **Worcester engine shed, 1964.** The view is of the shed nearest to the line from Shrub Hill to Droitwich; it was the former goods engine shed, which had three through roads with the eastern shed wall built on a curve. By the time of this picture, the larger shed had been demolished. No.7025 *Sudeley Castle* waits its next turn, probably one of the expresses to London, while 0-6-0PT No.8415 would be performing local shunting. '8100' class 2-6-2T No.8104 is just visible inside. The extractor cowls are still intact, soon they would be removed. Worcester shed officially closed to steam in 1965.

A J Booth

Below: **Servicing facilities at Worcester shed, 1964.** No.6980 *Llanrumney Hall* has just finished having its tender replenished from the mechanical coaler behind it. In 1942, £3,720 was spent on this machinery to replace the existing facility. In early 1949 the shed was witness to a curious incident. The LNER Beyer-Garrett engine, No. 69999, had arrived for banking duties at the Lickey incline the wrong way round and needed to be turned. It arrived here only to find that the turntable – not surprisingly – was too small! The triangle of lines was utilised to perform the manoeuvre.

M Mensing

Distance Box to Box (M)	(C)	NAME OF BOX	Weekdays Opened at Mondays	Other Days	Closed at	Sundays Opened at	Closed at	Whether provided with Switch
M—	C—	Oxford Station South	—	Open continuously		—	—	Yes
—	18	Oxford Station North	—	Open continuously		—	—	No
—	25	Oxford North Junction	—	Open continuously		—	—	Yes
1	53	Wolvercot Siding	—	Open continuously		—	—	Yes
—	64	Wolvercot Junction	—	Open continuously		—	—	No
—	71	Yarnton Junction	—	Open continuously		—	—	Yes
3	3	Handborough	4.15 a.m.			6.15 p.m.	2. 0 p.m. / 8.45 p.m.B	Yes
6	21	Charlbury	5.30 a.m.	—	—	—	2. 0 p.m.	Yes
3	60	Ascott-under-Wychwood	—	Open continuously		—	—	No
1	20	Shipton	12. 0 noon	12. 0 noon	3. 0 p.m. (or as required for traffic purposes)	—	—	Yes
1	37	Bruern Crossing	—	Open continuously		—	—	No
1	50	Kingham	5. 0 a.m.	—	—	—	10. 0 p.m.	Yes
2	57	Adlestrop	8. 0 a.m.	7. 0 a.m. / 7. 0 a.m.	4. 0 p.m.SX / 2.20 p.m.SO	—	—	Yes
4	14	Moreton-in-Marsh	5. 0 a.m.	—	—	—	8.45 p.m.	Yes
3	20	Blockley	—	Open continuously		—	—	No
2	1	Chipping Campden	—	Open continuously		—	—	No
3	55	Honeybourne (South Loop)	5.30 a.m.	—	—	—	2. 0 p.m.	Yes
—	75	Honeybourne Station South	5. 0 a.m.	—	—	—	11.30 p.m.X	Yes
—	34	Honeybourne Station North	—	Open continuously		—	—	Yes
—	—	Honeybourne West Loop	—	Open continuously		—	—	Yes
—	—	Honeybourne East Loop	5.30 a.m.	—	—	—	11.30 p.m.X	Yes
2	30	Littleton and Badsey	—	Open continuously		—	—	No
1	1	Aldington Siding	—	For traffic purposes only		—	—	Yes
1	22	Evesham South	4.20 a.m.	—	—	8.30 p.m.	8. 0 a.m. / 11.10 p.m.	Yes
—	39	Evesham North	6. 0 a.m.	6. 0 a.m.	10. 0 p.m.	—	—	Yes
1	71	Charlton Siding	12. 0 noon	12. 0 noon	5. 0 p.m. D	—	—	Yes
—	71	Fladbury	10. 0 a.m.	10. 0 a.m. / 10. 0 a.m.	8.0 p.m.E SX / 6.30 p.m.SO	—	—	Yes
2	48	Pershore	6. 0 a.m.	—	—	—	11.15 p.m.	Yes
2	21	Stoulton	—	For traffic purpose only		—	—	Yes
2	42	Norton Junction	—	Open continuously		—	—	Yes
2	66	Worcester (Wylds Lane Junction)	—	Open continuously		—	—	Yes
—	29	Worcester (Goods Yard)	5. 0 a.m.	—	—	—	6. 0 a.m.	No
—	25	Worcester (Shrub Hill Station)	—	Open continuously		—	—	No
—	15	Worcester (Shrub Hill Junction)	—	Open continuously		—	—	No
—	21	Worcester (Tunnel Junction)	—	Open continuously		—	—	No
1	18½	Blackpole Sidings	—	For traffic purposes only		—	—	Yes
1	2	Fernhill Heath	5. 0 a.m.	—	—	—	9. 0 p.m.	Yes
3	13	Droitwich Spa	—	Open continuously		—	—	No
3	20½	Cutnall Green	6. 0 a.m.	—	—	—	6. 0 a.m.	Yes
1	51½	Elmley Lovett Sidings	—	For traffic purposes only		—	—	Yes
—	54	Hartlebury Station	—	Open continuously		—	—	No
—	24	Hartlebury Junction	5. 0 a.m.	—	—	—	6.30 p.m.	Yes
3	2	Kidderminster Junction	—	Open continuously		—	—	Yes
—	23	Kidderminster Station	—	Open continuously		—	—	Yes
3	10	Churchill and Blakedown	—	Open continuously		—	—	Yes
1	66½	Hagley	6. 0 a.m.	—	—	—	2. 0 p.m.	Yes
1	52	Stourbridge Junction (South Box)	5. 0 a.m.	—	—	—	11.50 p.m. U	Yes
—	17½	Stourbridge Jn. (Middle Box)	—	Open continuously		—	—	Yes
—	29½	Stourbridge Junction (North Box)	—	Open continuously		—	—	No
—	33½	Stourbridge Junction (Engine Shed)	—	Open continuously		—	—	Yes
—	—	Worcester (Rainbow Hill Junction)	—	Open continuously		—	—	Yes
—	31	Worcester (Foregate Street)	7. 0 a.m.	7. 0 a.m.	11.15 p.m.V	—	—	Yes

B—Or after 6.40 p.m. Worcester has cleared.
D—Or after 5.0 p.m. Charlton Freight has cleared.
E—Provided 4.35 p.m. Chipping Campden Freight has cleared.
U—Or as ordered by Control.
V—Or until 10.55 p.m. (SX) Great Malvern and 10.10 p.m. (SO) Hereford have cleared.
X—Closed on Sundays 2.0 p.m. until 10.0 p.m.

Acknowledgements

This volume would not have seen the light of day if it hadn't been for the help and support of a large number of people and institutions. Special mention must be made of Stephen Mourton, Audie Baker, Roger Carpenter, the late Jim Peden, the Blencowe brothers and Tim Bryan at 'Steam' in Swindon. Public libraries have been a great source of information especially the local studies sections in Oxford, Worcester and Wolverhampton. Various societies have also helped, namely Signalling Record Society and the L&NWR Society. I am indebted to various pubs and tea rooms in North Oxfordshire and Worcestershire for sustaining me on my quest. The organisation and personnel at Kidderminster Railway Museum have been invaluable. The book, 'Great Western Lines & Landscapes' by Alan Bennett was a particular source of inspiration for the scenario for this volume in contrast to the industrial nature of volume two. Photographic credits, as far as possible to tell, have been appended to the appropriate captions.

While every effort has been made to obtain permission from owners of copyright materials reproduced herein, the publisher would like to apologise for any omissions and will be pleased to incorporate missing acknowledgements in any future editions.

Bibliography

The following, as well as numerous other books and magazines, were consulted and may contain more details of a particular area:

The Oxford, Worcester and Wolverhampton Railway *S C Jenkins & H I Quayle.*

The Oxford, Worcester and Wolverhampton Railway *John Boynton.*

Track layout diagrams of the GWR (section 28) *R A Cooke.*

Train Formations & Carriage Workings of the GWR *W S Becket.*

Heart of the GWR and several other books by *Adrian Vaughan.*

Stratford on Avon Branch *Audie Baker.*

Railway Magazines from 1904-1957.

BRILL, GWR Journal, BR Journal etc.

A large number of books on the health and imagery of Victorian England from Oxford library.

If any reader has pictures of the Carriage & Wagon works in Worcester, trains on the Vinegar Branch or of the halts at Mickleton, Astwood or Blackpole, the author would be very interested in talking to you. Pictures of trains splitting or being assembled at Worcester seem to have eluded him too – could you help fill this gap please?

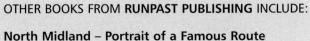
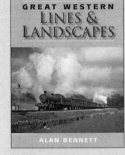

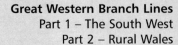